# A Beginner's Guide To

# GENERATIONAL WEALTH

## NEW AND EXPANDED EDITION



**Sherique Simms-Di**

Author | Educator | Generational Wealth Advocate

Sherique Simms-Dill

Nassau, New Providence

Bahamas

email:charisnasimms@yahoo.com

# Table of Contents

# DEDICATION

To my beloved children—**Joden, Jyelle, and Jendayia**—may you always walk in wisdom, discipline, and courage, building a legacy that outlives you. You are my greatest reminder of why generational wealth matters.

To my readers, supporters, and every family striving for financial freedom—this book is for you. May it inspire you to break cycles, create new traditions of abundance, and lay the foundation for generations yet to come.

And to all who dare to think beyond themselves, thank you for proving that true wealth is not just about money, but about vision, impact, and legacy.

# The Family Legacy Pledge

## A Commitment to Building Generational Wealth

Today, I make a decision that has the power to change not only my life but the lives of generations yet to come.

I choose to become a faithful steward of every resource entrusted to me.

I choose wisdom over impulse. I choose discipline over procrastination. I choose planning over uncertainty. I choose ownership over unnecessary consumption. I choose to build a legacy rather than simply earn a living. I acknowledge that wealth is more than money.

It is faith. It is character. It is integrity. It is knowledge. It is generosity. It is opportunity. It is the responsibility to leave those who come after me in a better position than I found them.

Beginning today, I commit to learning continuously, saving consistently, investing wisely, managing debt responsibly, protecting my family, and making financial decisions that reflect my values and long-term vision.

I will no longer allow fear, doubt, poor habits, or past mistakes to define my financial future. Instead, I will view every dollar as a tool, every opportunity as a blessing, and every wise decision as another brick in the foundation of my family's legacy.

I will teach the next generation the principles of financial stewardship, hard work, generosity, responsibility, and perseverance, understanding that the greatest inheritance I can leave is not merely wealth, but the wisdom to preserve and multiply it.

I understand that building generational wealth is not accomplished in a single day. It is built through thousands of faithful decisions made over a lifetime. I accept that there will be challenges. There will be setbacks. There will be lessons to learn.

But I choose to remain committed to the vision. I will celebrate progress rather than perfection. I will remain focused on purpose rather than appearances. I will seek wisdom before wealth and character before success. I recognize that my financial journey is not only about me.

The choices I make today will influence my children, my grandchildren, and generations I may never meet. May my life become an example of faithful stewardship. May my work create opportunity. May my generosity inspire others. May my legacy strengthen my family. May my faith guide every financial decision I make. And may future generations rise because I chose to begin.

**Today, I choose to become the generation that changes everything.**

**Today, I begin building a legacy that will outlive me.**

**Signature:** ______________________________

**Date:** __________________________________

# My Legacy Statement

With the prompt:

*"If my great-grandchildren were to describe my life 100 years from now, I hope they would say..."*

# Introduction

## Welcome to Your Journey Toward Generational Wealth

Money has the power to change lives—but wealth has the power to change generations.

Many people spend their entire lives working hard, earning a paycheck, paying bills, and hoping that one day they will have enough to retire comfortably. Yet despite years of dedication and sacrifice, they often leave little behind for the next generation beyond memories and unpaid bills. This cycle has continued in countless families for decades, not because people lack ambition or intelligence, but because they were never taught how to build, protect, and transfer wealth.

*A Beginner's Guide to Generational Wealth* was written to change that.

This book is not about becoming an overnight millionaire or chasing the latest investment trend. It is about building a strong financial foundation that can support not only your life, but also the lives of your children, grandchildren, and future generations. It is about making intentional decisions today that will create opportunities for tomorrow.

Generational wealth is more than the amount of money in a bank account. It is the legacy of financial wisdom, responsible stewardship, education, ownership, discipline, and opportunity that is passed from one generation to the next. Families who build lasting wealth understand that true prosperity is not measured solely by what they earn—it is measured by what they preserve, multiply, and leave behind.

Whether you are just beginning your financial journey or working to strengthen your current financial position, this book will provide practical guidance to help you move forward with confidence. Throughout these pages, you will learn how to transform your mindset about money, develop healthy financial habits, manage debt wisely, create positive cash flow, build valuable assets, protect your family's future, prepare for retirement, and establish a lasting legacy.

Along the way, you will also discover an important truth: wealth begins long before the first investment is made. It begins with the decisions we make every day—how we think, how we spend, how we save, how we plan, and how we teach those who come after us.

One of the unique aspects of this book is its emphasis on stewardship. Money is a tool, not a destination. When managed with wisdom, integrity, and purpose, it becomes a resource that allows us to care for our families, invest in our communities, support meaningful causes, and create opportunities for future generations. Financial success and faithful stewardship can work hand in hand.

Throughout this book, you will find practical examples, reflection questions, action steps, and coaching insights designed to help you move beyond simply reading about wealth to actively building it. The goal is not just to increase your financial knowledge but to help you develop lasting financial habits that produce measurable results over time.

Remember that building generational wealth is not a race. It is a lifelong journey. Every dollar saved, every debt reduced, every investment made, every lesson taught to your children, and every wise financial decision becomes another brick in the foundation of your family's future. Small, consistent actions often produce extraordinary results over time.

As you read, I encourage you to keep an open mind. Some of the ideas in these chapters may challenge long-held beliefs about money. Others may inspire you to take steps you have never considered before. Embrace the learning process, remain committed to your goals, and remember that lasting wealth is built through patience, consistency, discipline, and informed decision-making.

The companion **Generational Wealth Planner** has been designed to work alongside this book, giving you a practical place to apply the principles you learn. As you complete exercises, track your progress, set goals, and develop financial habits, you will be transforming knowledge into action—because understanding wealth is valuable, but building it requires intentional effort.

No matter where you are today, your financial story is still being written.

The choices you make from this moment forward have the power to change your future—and perhaps the future of generations yet to come.

Let's begin building your legacy, one wise financial decision at a time.

# PART I – Building the Foundation

# Chapter One
# What Is Generational Wealth?

*"A good person leaves an inheritance for their children's children..."*

— Proverbs 13:22 (NIV)

## More Than Money

When many people hear the word *wealth*, they immediately think of millionaires, luxury cars, private jets, expensive homes, and overflowing bank accounts. Society has conditioned us to associate wealth with outward displays of success and material possessions. While financial abundance can certainly provide comfort and opportunity, true generational wealth goes far beyond the balance in a bank account.

Generational wealth is the intentional process of building financial resources, valuable assets, knowledge, wisdom, and opportunities that can be passed from one generation to the next. It is about creating a legacy that continues to benefit your family long after you are gone.

Contrary to popular belief, generational wealth is not reserved for the rich. Every family has the ability to begin building wealth, regardless of where they start. While some may begin with larger financial resources than others, every family can begin laying a foundation through consistent saving, wise investing, responsible stewardship, and financial education.

Building generational wealth is less about how much money you earn and more about how intentionally you manage what you have.

## Wealth vs. Income

One of the greatest financial misconceptions is believing that earning a high income automatically makes someone wealthy.

Income is the money you receive from working. Wealth is what remains after you have managed, saved, invested, and protected your money over time.

A person earning $40,000 a year who consistently saves, invests, and lives below their means may accumulate greater wealth than someone earning $200,000 a year who spends every dollar they make.

This distinction is important because many people spend years pursuing larger paychecks without ever developing the habits that lead to lasting financial security.

Income provides opportunity.

Wealth provides freedom.

Generational wealth provides opportunity and freedom for those who come after you.

## Breaking the Cycle

Many families unknowingly pass down financial struggles from one generation to the next. Children often grow up repeating the money habits they observed at home. If budgeting was never discussed, they may never learn to budget. If saving was not prioritized, they may struggle to save. If debt became a way of life, borrowing may seem normal.

These patterns are rarely intentional.

Most parents simply teach what they themselves were taught.

The encouraging news is that cycles can be broken.

Every generation has the opportunity to become the turning point.

Perhaps your parents were unable to save because they lived paycheck to paycheck. Perhaps no one ever spoke to you about investing, retirement planning, or estate planning. Perhaps financial hardship has been a recurring theme throughout your family's history.

That history does not have to become your future.

Someone must become the first generation to say:

*"The cycle stops with me."*

Generational wealth begins with one person making different decisions.

## The Four Pillars of Generational Wealth

Building lasting wealth rests upon four essential pillars.

**Pillar One: Financial Knowledge**

Knowledge is one of the greatest assets a family can possess. Learning how money works empowers you to make wise financial decisions and avoid costly mistakes. Financial education should never stop. The more you understand about saving, investing, taxes, insurance, credit, and estate planning, the better equipped you become to build lasting wealth.

**Pillar Two: Financial Discipline**

Knowledge alone is not enough.

Many people know they should save, but fail to do so. Others understand debt but continue making poor financial decisions.

Discipline transforms knowledge into daily habits.

It is choosing today's wisdom over today's impulse.

**Pillar Four: Legacy**

Perhaps the most overlooked pillar is legacy.

Many people spend decades building wealth but never prepare the next generation to manage it.

Without financial education, communication, and proper planning, wealth can disappear within a single generation.

A true legacy includes:

- Financial resources.

- Financial wisdom.
- Strong values.
- Faith and integrity.
- Education.
- Family traditions.
- A vision for future generations.

Money may open doors.

Wisdom keeps them open.

**Pillar Three: Asset Building**

True wealth is created through ownership.

Assets are resources that grow in value or generate income over time. These may include real estate, businesses, investments, intellectual property, retirement accounts, royalties, and other income-producing resources.

Assets continue working even when you are not.

The goal is to own things that increase your financial strength rather than continually purchasing items that lose value.

## You Do Not Have to Be Wealthy to Begin

One of the greatest myths about generational wealth is believing you must already have significant wealth before you can start building it.

Nothing could be further from the truth.

Every successful financial journey begins with a single decision.

You may begin with a modest salary.

You may still be paying off debt.

You may be raising children on a limited income.

You may have made financial mistakes in the past.

None of these circumstances disqualify you from creating a better future.

What matters most is your willingness to begin.

History is filled with individuals who built extraordinary legacies not because they started with abundance, but because they developed consistency, patience, discipline, and vision.

Your current financial situation is your starting point—not your destination.

## A Legacy Worth Leaving

Imagine your grandchildren graduating from university without overwhelming student debt because you planned ahead.

Imagine your children inheriting a home instead of financial burdens.

Imagine leaving behind investments, businesses, insurance benefits, valuable life lessons, and family traditions that continue blessing your descendants for decades.

Now imagine something even greater.

Imagine your family becoming known for wisdom, generosity, integrity, and responsible stewardship.

That is the true power of generational wealth.

It is not simply about leaving money.

It is about leaving opportunities.

It is about leaving knowledge.

It is about leaving hope.

And it all begins with one decision:

To become the generation that changes everything.

## Wealth Reflection

Generational wealth begins long before your bank account reaches a certain number. It starts with a decision to think differently, live intentionally, and prepare for a future beyond your own lifetime. The legacy you build today can become the foundation upon which future generations stand.

## Action Steps

☐ Write down what generational wealth means to you and your family.

☐ Identify one financial habit you want to change this month.

☐ Discuss one financial goal with your spouse, children, or a trusted family member.

☐ Begin a "Legacy Journal" to record the financial lessons you want to pass on to future generations.

☐ Commit to reading one chapter of this book each week and applying at least one lesson.

## ⍰Coach's Corner

You don't have to be born into wealth to create it. Every family that enjoys financial security today began with someone who decided to break old patterns and build something better. Perhaps that person is you. Don't underestimate the impact of the choices you make today. Years from now, your children and grandchildren may enjoy opportunities because you chose to start—even when the journey seemed difficult.

## Planner Connection

Now that you understand what generational wealth truly is, it's time to begin defining your own vision. In the Generational Wealth Planner, complete the Family Legacy Vision, Financial Goals Assessment, and Generational Wealth Roadmap to begin creating a clear picture of the future you want to build.

# Chapter Two

# Breaking the Money Is Evil Mindset

## "For the love of money is a root of all kinds of evil..."

## — 1 Timothy 6:10 (NIV)

## The Beliefs We Inherit About Money

Long before we earn our first paycheck, open our first bank account, or make our first investment, we begin forming beliefs about money.

These beliefs often come from our parents, grandparents, teachers, religious communities, culture, and personal experiences. We observe how money is discussed at the dinner table, how bills are paid, how financial hardships are handled, and whether wealth is viewed as a blessing or a burden.

Some people grow up hearing:

- "Money doesn't grow on trees."
- "Rich people are greedy."
- "People like us never get ahead."
- "The wealthy must have cheated to get there."
- "If I have more, someone else must have less."

Although these statements may seem harmless, they quietly shape our attitudes toward money. Over time, they become internal beliefs that influence our decisions, our confidence, and even the opportunities we pursue.

If we believe wealth is wrong, we may unconsciously avoid creating it.

If we believe success is reserved for others, we may never fully pursue our own potential.

The first step toward generational wealth is recognizing the beliefs we carry and asking ourselves an important question:

Are these beliefs true, or have I simply accepted them because they were repeated so often?

## Understanding What the Bible Really Says

One of the most misunderstood verses in Scripture is:

*"For the love of money is a root of all kinds of evil."*

Notice what the verse does **not** say.

It does not say that **money** is evil.

It says that **the love of money**—placing wealth above God, people, integrity, and purpose—can lead to destructive choices.

Money itself is neither good nor bad.

Money is a tool.

In the hands of a generous person, money can feed families, educate children, build schools, support ministries, provide healthcare, and create opportunities.

In the hands of someone driven by greed, the same money can become a source of exploitation, dishonesty, and corruption.

The issue is never the money.

The issue is the heart of the person managing it.

## Wealth Is Stewardship

Everything we possess ultimately belongs to God. We are not owners in the absolute sense—we are stewards entrusted with resources for a season.

A faithful steward asks:

- How can I manage my finances wisely?
- How can I provide for my family?
- How can I prepare for future generations?
- How can I use my resources to help others?
- How can my wealth glorify God?

When we understand stewardship, wealth becomes a responsibility rather than a status symbol.

Instead of asking, "How much can I accumulate?"

We begin asking, "How wisely can I manage what has been entrusted to me?"

That shift changes everything.

## Poverty Is Not a Requirement for Holiness

Throughout history, some people have mistakenly believed that financial struggle is a sign of spiritual devotion, while prosperity is evidence of selfishness.

The Bible presents a more balanced picture.

Many faithful individuals were entrusted with significant resources because they managed them wisely and remained faithful to God's purpose.

Their wealth enabled them to provide employment, support their communities, care for their families, and advance God's work.

Scripture consistently teaches responsibility, generosity, honesty, diligence, and wise planning—not reckless spending or irresponsible accumulation.

God is far more interested in how we manage wealth than how much we possess.

## The Cost of Limiting Beliefs

Negative beliefs about money often produce behaviors that keep people financially stuck.

For example:

If you believe investing is only for wealthy people, you may never begin investing.

If you believe business ownership is too risky, you may never pursue entrepreneurship.

If you believe you will always struggle financially, you may stop looking for opportunities altogether.

Our beliefs shape our expectations.

Our expectations influence our decisions.

Our decisions determine our outcomes.

Changing your financial future begins by changing the story you tell yourself about money.

## A Healthy Wealth Mindset

Developing a healthy relationship with money means replacing fear and guilt with wisdom and purpose.

Instead of saying:

"I'll never have enough."

Say:

"I can learn to manage what I have wisely."

Instead of saying:

"Wealth is only for other people."

Say:

"With knowledge, discipline, and consistency, I can build lasting wealth."

Instead of saying:

"Money changes people."

Say:

"Money reveals character. I choose to use it with integrity."

These small shifts in thinking create powerful changes over time.

## Wealth with Purpose

Generational wealth is never about impressing others.

It is about creating choices.

Choices to educate your children.

Choices to care for aging parents.

Choices to support charitable causes.

Choices to invest in your community.

Choices to weather unexpected financial storms without fear.

When wealth has a purpose, it becomes a tool for service rather than a symbol of success.

The question is no longer:

"How much money do I want to make?"

The better question is:

"What kind of impact do I want my resources to have?"

That perspective transforms wealth into legacy.

## Begin with One New Belief

You do not need to change every financial habit overnight.

Start by replacing one limiting belief with one empowering truth.

Then let that new belief shape your choices.

Small changes in thinking lead to better decisions.

Better decisions lead to healthier financial habits.

Healthy habits build lasting wealth.

And lasting wealth creates opportunities for generations yet to come.

## Wealth Reflection

Your financial future is influenced not only by the money you earn but also by the beliefs you hold. Take time to examine the messages you have accepted about money and consider whether they are helping or hindering your journey toward financial freedom and generational wealth.

## Action Steps

☐ Write down three beliefs about money that you learned growing up.

☐ Identify whether each belief has helped or limited your financial growth.

☐ Replace one limiting belief with a healthier, empowering statement.

☐ Read 1 Timothy 6:6–10 and reflect on the difference between money and the love of money.

☐ Share one positive financial lesson with a family member this week.

---

## ◈Coach's Corner

Many people inherit financial struggles without ever inheriting financial education. Don't feel discouraged if no one taught you how to build wealth. The fact that you are reading this book means you are already changing the direction of your family's future. Every new principle you learn is another brick in the foundation of your legacy. Keep building.

---

## Planner Connection

In your Generational Wealth Planner, complete the Money Mindset Assessment, Limiting Beliefs Exercise, and Personal Wealth Affirmations. These activities will help you identify old financial patterns and begin replacing them with beliefs that support wise stewardship and long-term wealth building.

# Chapter Three

# Financial Habits That Build or Break Wealth

## "Whoever can be trusted with very little can also be trusted with much..."

## — Luke 16:10 (NIV)

## Wealth Is Built Through Habits

Many people believe that wealth is created by one lucky break, a high-paying job, or a winning lottery ticket. While unexpected opportunities can certainly improve a person's financial situation, lasting wealth is rarely built overnight. Instead, it is built through the small financial decisions we make every day.

Every purchase. Every bill paid on time. Every dollar saved. Every investment made. Every unnecessary expense avoided. These daily choices may seem insignificant in the moment, but over months, years, and decades, they shape our financial future. Successful people are not simply people who earn more. They are often people who have developed better financial habits.

The encouraging news is that habits can be learned, improved, and strengthened over time.

## Habits Shape Your Financial Future

Consider two individuals who earn the exact same salary.

One spends every dollar as soon as it is received, relies heavily on credit cards, saves very little, and makes purchases based on emotions.

The other follows a budget, saves consistently, avoids unnecessary debt, and invests a portion of every paycheck.

Five years later, their financial lives will likely look very different—not because of how much they earned, but because of how they managed what they earned.

Your habits determine whether money becomes a temporary visitor or a lifelong servant.

## Seven Habits That Keep People Financially Stuck

### 1. Living Beyond Your Means

One of the most common financial mistakes is spending more than you earn.

Many people increase their lifestyle every time their income increases. A larger salary leads to a larger house, a newer car, more subscriptions, more dining out, and more unnecessary spending.

Instead of building wealth, they build bigger monthly expenses.

True wealth often begins by living below your means, not above them.

### 2. Not Having a Budget

A budget is not a punishment.

It is a financial plan.

Without a budget, money tends to disappear without explanation. Small purchases accumulate, bills become overwhelming, and savings are often forgotten.

A budget simply tells your money where to go instead of wondering where it went.

### 3. Saving Only What Is Left Over

Many people promise themselves they will save whatever remains at the end of the month.

Unfortunately, there is often very little left.

Wealthy individuals typically reverse this process.

They save first.

Then they live on what remains.

This simple shift creates consistency and discipline.

**4. Depending on Debt**

Debt should never become a lifestyle.

While certain types of debt can help build assets, constantly relying on borrowed money for everyday expenses often creates financial stress and limits future opportunities.

Borrow only when it moves you toward a meaningful financial goal—not simply to satisfy today's wants.

**5. Ignoring Financial Education**

Schools teach many valuable subjects, but many people complete their education without learning how money truly works.

Financial education is one of the greatest investments you can make:

- Books
- Courses
- Seminars
- Mentors
- Podcasts

Every lesson you learn increases your ability to make wiser financial decisions. Knowledge compounds just like money.

**6. Trying to Impress Others**

One of the quickest ways to delay financial freedom is constantly trying to appear successful.

Designer clothing.

Luxury vehicles.

Expensive vacations.

The latest technology.

None of these necessarily indicate wealth.

Many truly wealthy individuals live modestly while investing quietly behind the scenes.

Remember:

Appearances are temporary.

Assets create lasting security.

**7. Waiting for "Someday"**

Many people postpone financial planning because they believe they will begin once they earn more money.

"I'll save when I get a raise."

"I'll invest after the children grow up."

"I'll start next year."

Unfortunately, tomorrow often becomes years.

The best time to begin building wealth is today—even if your first step is small.

## Seven Habits That Build Wealth

Now let's replace unhealthy habits with healthier ones.

**Habit 1: Spend with Purpose**

Before making purchases, ask yourself:

*"Does this purchase move me closer to or further from my financial goals?"*

Intentional spending creates intentional wealth.

**Habit 2: Pay Yourself First**

Treat savings like any other monthly bill.

When you receive income, immediately set aside a percentage for savings or investments before spending on anything else.

This simple habit has transformed countless financial lives.

**Habit 3: Track Your Spending**

You cannot improve what you do not measure.

Recording your expenses reveals spending patterns that often go unnoticed.

Awareness leads to better decisions.

**Habit 4: Build an Emergency Fund**

Unexpected expenses are part of life.

Medical emergencies.

Vehicle repairs.

Home maintenance.

Job loss.

An emergency fund protects you from turning every unexpected expense into debt.

**Habit 5: Invest in Yourself**

Your greatest financial asset is not your bank account.

It is your ability to earn, learn, and grow:

- Develop new skills
- Earn certifications
- Read books
- Attend workshops
- Increase your value

The more valuable your skills become, the greater your opportunities may become.

**Habit 6: Practice Contentment**

Contentment does not mean a lack of ambition.

It means appreciating what you have while responsibly working toward what you desire.

Gratitude often leads to wiser financial decisions than comparison.

**Habit 7: Think Generationally**

Before making major financial decisions, ask yourself:

*"How will this decision affect my family five, ten, or twenty years from now?"*

Generational thinkers make decisions with the future in mind.

**Small Habits Create Extraordinary Results**

Imagine saving just $10 every day.

At first, it may seem insignificant.

Over time, however, those small amounts accumulate into thousands of dollars.

Now imagine investing those savings consistently over many years.

Small habits, repeated consistently, often produce extraordinary outcomes.

The same principle applies to debt.

Small unnecessary purchases repeated every day can quietly consume thousands of dollars each year.

Success is rarely found in dramatic moments.

It is found in consistent daily choices.

## Your Financial Habits Become Your Family's Habits

Children learn more from what they observe than from what they are told.

If they see budgeting, saving, generosity, planning, and responsible spending, they are more likely to develop those same habits.

Likewise, if they see constant financial stress, impulsive spending, and unmanaged debt, they may unknowingly repeat those patterns as adults.

Remember:

You are not only building your own financial future.

You are modeling financial behavior for future generations.

That may become one of the greatest gifts you ever leave behind.

---

## Legacy Builder Spotlight

**Warren Buffett: The Power of Consistency**

Warren Buffett, one of the world's most successful investors, did not become wealthy overnight. His success came from decades of disciplined investing, patience, and allowing compound growth to work in his favor.

Despite his immense wealth, Buffett has long been known for living modestly, remaining in the same home for many years, avoiding unnecessary extravagance, and making thoughtful financial decisions.

His life demonstrates an important lesson:

**Extraordinary wealth is often the result of ordinary habits practiced consistently over a lifetime.**

## Wealth Reflection

Your financial habits are quietly shaping your future every single day. While one poor decision is unlikely to determine your destiny, repeated choices create powerful patterns. The habits you build today can become the foundation of financial freedom tomorrow.

**Action Steps**

☐ Review your spending over the past 30 days.

☐ Identify three habits that are helping you build wealth.

☐ Identify three habits that are slowing your financial progress.

☐ Create one new financial habit to practice consistently this month.

☐ Share one positive money habit with your children or another family member.

## ⍰ Coach's Corner

People often look for a secret formula to becoming wealthy, but there isn't one. Wealth is usually the result of simple habits practiced with remarkable consistency. Don't become discouraged because your progress feels slow. Every dollar you save, every debt you reduce, every wise purchase you make, and every investment in your future is another step toward the legacy you're building. Stay faithful to the process—the results will come.

## Planner Connection

In your Generational Wealth Planner, complete the 30-Day Spending Tracker, Monthly Budget Worksheet, Financial Habits Assessment, Savings Challenge, and Wealth-Building Habit Tracker. These tools will help you turn today's lessons into daily actions that strengthen your financial future.

You can start off with Five Hundred or One Thousand Dollars. Every month you can add more funds to it until you reach your goal.

## Benefits of having an Emergency Fund

When you have an emergency fund, it significantly decreases your chances of racking up your credit card bill or having to take out personal loans from banking institutions. These facilitators charge a high rate of interest for their services. Also, the interest is compounded. Small urgencies such as purchasing a pre-owned car, house repairs, small medical bills, car repairs, tax bills, etc. can be paid out of pocket. Why whip up debt by borrowing for these small matters?

You can avoid unnecessarily borrowing money from the banks by building a cash cushion.

*We want to leave a legacy of benefits for our children, not bills! Sherique Dill*

# Chapter Four

# Saving and Borrowing Wisely

## "The plans of the diligent lead surely to abundance, but everyone who is hasty comes only to poverty."

## — Proverbs 21:5 (ESV)

## Every Dollar Has a Job

One of the greatest financial lessons you can learn is that every dollar you earn should have a purpose.

Too often, people receive their income and spend it without a plan. By the end of the month, they wonder where their money went and why they have nothing left to save.

Wealth builders think differently.

Before they spend a dollar, they decide what that dollar is meant to accomplish.

Some dollars are meant to pay bills.

Some are meant to provide for today's needs.

Some are meant to protect against emergencies.

Others are meant to grow through investments.

When every dollar has a purpose, money begins working for you instead of disappearing without direction.

## Why Saving Matters

Saving is more than putting money into a bank account.

It is creating financial stability.

Savings provide peace of mind during uncertain times. Unexpected expenses are no longer financial disasters when you have prepared in advance.

Saving also creates opportunity.

A person with savings can take advantage of business opportunities, invest in education, purchase assets, or weather difficult seasons without relying heavily on debt.

Saving is not about fear.

It is about preparation.

As Benjamin Franklin wisely said:

"By failing to prepare, you are preparing to fail."

Preparation is one of the greatest forms of financial wisdom.

## Pay Yourself First

Many people save only what remains after paying everyone else.

Unfortunately, very little often remains.

One of the most effective wealth-building habits is paying yourself first.

This simply means setting aside a portion of your income immediately after you are paid.

Even if you begin with 5% or 10%, consistency matters far more than the amount.

Saving first communicates that your future is just as important as your present.

Over time, those consistent deposits become one of the strongest foundations of financial security.

## Build an Emergency Fund

Life is unpredictable:

- Vehicles break down
- Homes require repairs
- Medical emergencies occur
- Employment situations change

Without savings, these events often lead to borrowing money at high interest rates.

An emergency fund acts as a financial cushion.

Financial experts generally recommend building enough savings to cover three to six months of essential living expenses. If that goal feels overwhelming, begin with a smaller milestone such as $500 or $1,000. Reaching those first goals builds confidence and momentum.

Remember:

Small beginnings often lead to remarkable results.

## Saving for Goals

Not every savings account should serve the same purpose.

Creating separate savings goals helps you remain focused and disciplined.

Examples include:

- Emergency savings
- Home ownership
- Education

- Retirement
- Business startup
- Family vacation
- Vehicle replacement
- Investment opportunities

Giving each savings goal a name transforms it from abstract money into a meaningful purpose.

People tend to protect money when they know exactly why they are saving it.

## Understanding Borrowing

Borrowing is often viewed as either completely good or completely bad.

The truth lies somewhere in the middle.

Borrowing is simply a financial tool.

Like any tool, it can be used wisely or carelessly.

Used responsibly, borrowing can help purchase assets that appreciate in value or increase your earning potential.

Used irresponsibly, borrowing can create years of financial stress.

The key question is not:

*"Should I borrow?"*

The better question is:

*"Will this borrowing improve my financial future?"*

## Good Debt vs. Bad Debt

Understanding the difference between productive debt and destructive debt is essential.

### Good Debt

Good debt is generally used to acquire something that has the potential to increase in value or generate future income.

Examples include:

- Purchasing a primary home (when affordable)
- Investing in education or professional training
- Starting or expanding a business
- Purchasing equipment that increases income
- Acquiring investment property

These decisions should always be made carefully, with realistic repayment plans.

### Bad Debt

Bad debt is usually incurred to purchase items that quickly lose value or satisfy temporary wants.

Examples include:

- High-interest credit card balances
- Impulse purchases
- Expensive vacations financed through loans
- Luxury items beyond your financial means
- Constant financing of consumer goods

These types of debt often reduce future financial flexibility without creating lasting value.

## Borrow with Wisdom

Before borrowing money, ask yourself five important questions:

1. Do I truly need this?
2. Can I comfortably afford the monthly payment?

3. Will this purchase increase my long-term financial position?
4. What is the total cost after interest?
5. If my income changed unexpectedly, could I still repay this loan?

These questions encourage thoughtful decisions rather than emotional ones.

## The Cost of Interest

Interest can become either your greatest financial ally or one of your greatest financial obstacles.

When you save and invest, compound interest allows your money to grow over time.

When you carry expensive debt, interest works in the opposite direction, increasing the amount you owe.

Understanding this difference is one of the most valuable financial lessons anyone can learn.

Whenever possible, position yourself so that interest works **for you** rather than against you.

## Delayed Gratification

One characteristic shared by many financially successful people is the willingness to wait.

Rather than purchasing immediately, they save.

Rather than financing unnecessary items, they prepare.

Rather than seeking instant satisfaction, they think about future freedom.

Delayed gratification is not about denying yourself enjoyment.

It is about making choices today that create greater opportunities tomorrow.

Often, the ability to wait becomes one of the greatest advantages in building wealth.

## Legacy Begins with Preparation

Saving is not merely about accumulating money.

Borrowing wisely is not merely about managing debt.

Both are acts of preparation.

Every dollar you save strengthens your family's future.

Every wise borrowing decision protects future opportunities.

Every thoughtful financial choice becomes another brick in the foundation of your family's legacy.

Generational wealth is built through preparation long before it is recognized by others.

---

## Legacy Builder Spotlight

**Ingvar Kamprad: Saving with Purpose**

Ingvar Kamprad, the founder of IKEA, became one of the wealthiest entrepreneurs in the world, yet he was widely known for his frugal lifestyle. He flew economy class, drove modest vehicles, and believed that every unnecessary expense reduced resources that could be invested elsewhere.

His philosophy reminds us that wealth is not measured by extravagant spending but by wise stewardship. Saving consistently and spending intentionally allowed him to grow one of the world's most successful companies while maintaining financial discipline.

His example teaches an important lesson:

Building wealth is often less about how much you earn and more about how wisely you manage what you have.

## Wealth Reflection

Saving is an investment in your future, while borrowing is a responsibility that should always be approached with wisdom. Every financial decision you make today either strengthens or weakens the legacy you hope to leave behind.

## Action Steps

☐ Open or review your emergency savings account.

☐ Set one short-term and one long-term savings goal.

☐ List every outstanding loan and its interest rate.

☐ Identify one debt you can begin paying down more aggressively.

☐ Before making your next major purchase, apply the five borrowing questions from this chapter.

## ◈ Coach's Corner

One of the greatest financial freedoms comes from knowing you have prepared for life's unexpected moments. Don't be discouraged if your savings seem small today. Every deposit represents discipline, hope, and confidence in your future. Likewise, every wise decision to avoid unnecessary debt protects opportunities that your future self—and perhaps your children—will one day appreciate.

## Planner Connection

In your Generational Wealth Planner, complete the Emergency Fund Tracker, Savings Goals Worksheet, Debt Elimination Plan, Loan Comparison

Worksheet, and Financial Goals Timeline. These planning tools will help you transform today's financial decisions into long-term financial security.

# Chapter Five

# Mastering Cash Flow: The Lifeblood of Wealth

**"Be diligent to know the state of your flocks, and attend to your herds."**

**— Proverbs 27:23 (ESV)**

## What Is Cash Flow?

Imagine your finances as a river.

Money flows into your life through your salary, business income, rental properties, investments, royalties, pensions, or other sources of income.

At the same time, money flows out through housing, food, transportation, insurance, debt payments, entertainment, education, taxes, and everyday living expenses.

This constant movement of money is called **cash flow**.

Simply put:

**Cash Flow = Money Coming In – Money Going Out**

If more money comes in than goes out, you have **positive cash flow**.

If more money goes out than comes in, you have **negative cash flow**.

Positive cash flow creates opportunities.

Negative cash flow creates stress.

Understanding this simple principle is one of the most important financial skills you can develop.

## Why Income Alone Is Not Enough

Many people assume that earning more money automatically solves financial problems.

Unfortunately, that is not always true.

Imagine two individuals:

**Person A** earns $50,000 per year and spends $40,000.

**Person B** earns $150,000 per year but spends $160,000.

Although Person B earns three times as much money, Person A is in the stronger financial position because they have positive cash flow.

Income creates opportunity.

Cash flow determines whether you actually build wealth.

This is why many high-income earners still struggle financially, while others with more modest incomes steadily increase their net worth.

## Where Does Your Money Go?

One of the biggest financial surprises people experience is discovering how much money quietly disappears each month.

Small daily purchases often seem harmless.

A coffee here.

Lunch there.

A streaming subscription.

Impulse purchases.

Frequent online shopping.

Dining out several times each week.

Individually, these expenses may seem insignificant.

Together, they can quietly consume thousands of dollars each year.

The first step toward improving cash flow is becoming aware of where your money is actually going.

You cannot improve what you refuse to measure.

## The Difference Between Needs and Wants

Every financial decision involves a choice.

Needs are the essentials required for daily living:

- Housing
- Food
- Utilities
- Transportation
- Healthcare
- Basic clothing

Wants improve comfort and enjoyment but are not necessary for survival.

Examples include:

- Designer brands
- Luxury vehicles
- Frequent vacations
- Premium entertainment services
- Upgraded electronics

There is nothing wrong with enjoying life's blessings.

The challenge comes when wants consistently take priority over financial goals.

Generational wealth requires learning to balance present enjoyment with future security.

## Create a Spending Plan

Many people dislike the word **budget** because they associate it with restrictions.

Think of it differently.

A budget is simply a spending plan.

It gives every dollar an assignment before it is spent.

Instead of asking:

*"Where did my money go?"*

You begin asking:

*"Where do I want my money to go?"*

That simple shift puts you back in control.

A healthy spending plan should include:

- Giving
- Savings
- Investments
- Housing
- Utilities
- Food
- Transportation
- Insurance
- Debt payments

- Personal spending
- Entertainment

When your money has direction, your financial future gains direction as well.

## Increase the Gap

One of the simplest ways to improve cash flow is to increase the gap between income and expenses.

There are only two ways to accomplish this:

**Increase Your Income**

Consider ways to earn more through:

- Career advancement
- Professional certifications
- Starting a business
- Freelancing
- Consulting
- Selling digital products
- Rental properties
- Investments
- Royaltics
- Side hustles

Every additional income stream strengthens your financial resilience.

**Reduce Unnecessary Expenses**

Review your spending honestly.

Ask yourself:

- What subscriptions am I no longer using?
- What purchases are based on habit rather than need?

- Where can I negotiate better prices?
- What expenses can I reduce without lowering my quality of life?

Small savings repeated every month produce remarkable long-term results.

## Positive Cash Flow Creates Choices

When your income consistently exceeds your expenses, new opportunities begin to appear.

You can:

- Invest regularly.
- Build emergency savings.
- Purchase income-producing assets.
- Eliminate debt faster.
- Prepare for retirement.
- Help family members.
- Support charitable causes.
- Start a business.

Positive cash flow transforms money from a source of stress into a source of opportunity.

## Cash Flow Is the Engine of Generational Wealth

Think of cash flow as fuel for your financial engine.

Without positive cash flow:

You cannot consistently save.

You cannot consistently invest.

You cannot consistently build assets.

You cannot consistently leave wealth to future generations.

Every successful wealth-building strategy begins with positive cash flow.

This is why wealthy families often focus less on appearances and more on maintaining healthy financial margins.

## Make Your Money Work Harder

As your financial position improves, your goal should not simply be to earn more.

Your goal should be to make every dollar work harder.

Ask yourself:

- Can this money earn interest?
- Can it generate rental income?
- Can it purchase an appreciating asset?
- Can it fund a business?
- Can it create passive income?
- Can it improve my family's future?

Money that works creates freedom.

Money that sits idle loses opportunity.

## Cash Flow Is About Freedom

Ultimately, cash flow is not about numbers on a spreadsheet.

It is about freedom.

Freedom to make decisions without constant financial pressure.

Freedom to prepare for emergencies.

Freedom to pursue meaningful opportunities.

Freedom to give generously.

Freedom to leave your children with opportunities instead of financial burdens.

Positive cash flow is one of the strongest foundations upon which generational wealth is built.

---

# Legacy Builder Spotlight

**Robert Kiyosaki: Understanding the Flow of Money**

Author and entrepreneur Robert Kiyosaki popularized the idea that understanding cash flow is more important than simply earning a large income. Through his teachings, he encouraged millions of people to focus on acquiring assets that generate income rather than accumulating liabilities that consume it.

Whether readers agree with every aspect of his investment philosophy or not, one lesson remains valuable:

Financial freedom is achieved not merely by earning more, but by managing the flow of money wisely and building assets that continue to generate income over time.

---

# Wealth Reflection

Cash flow reveals the health of your finances. It shows whether your money is creating opportunities or creating stress. By becoming intentional about both your income and your expenses, you place yourself in a stronger position to build lasting wealth and provide future generations with greater financial security.

---

# Action Steps

☐ Track every dollar you spend for the next 30 days.

☐ Calculate your monthly cash flow by subtracting expenses from income.

☐ Identify three expenses you can reduce or eliminate.

☐ Identify one new way to increase your monthly income.

☐ Create a monthly spending plan that includes giving, saving, investing, and essential expenses.

---

## ⍰ Coach's Corner

Many people believe financial success begins with earning more money. In reality, it begins with managing the money you already have. Mastering cash flow is one of the most empowering financial skills you can develop because it gives you control over your finances instead of allowing your finances to control you. Small improvements made consistently can completely transform your financial future.

---

## Planner Connection

In your Generational Wealth Planner, complete the Monthly Cash Flow Statement, Income Tracker, Expense Tracker, Needs vs. Wants Worksheet, Subscription Audit, and Cash Flow Improvement Plan. These exercises will help you identify opportunities to strengthen your finances and create positive cash flow each month.

# PART II – Building Wealth

# Chapter Six

# Understanding Debt and Credit

## "The rich rule over the poor, and the borrower is servant to the lender."

## — Proverbs 22:7 (NIV)

## Debt Is a Tool—Not a Way of Life

Debt is one of the most misunderstood aspects of personal finance. Some people believe all debt is harmful and should be avoided at any cost, while others see borrowing as the solution to almost every financial need.

The truth lies somewhere between these extremes.

Debt is a financial tool. Like any tool, it can be used wisely or carelessly.

A hammer can build a home or break a window. The tool itself is not the problem—it is how it is used.

In the same way, debt can help create opportunity when used responsibly, or it can become a burden that limits financial freedom when used recklessly.

The goal is not simply to avoid debt.

The goal is to understand it, manage it wisely, and never allow it to control your future.

## Understanding Credit

Credit is your financial reputation.

It tells lenders how responsibly you have handled borrowed money in the past.

When you consistently pay your bills on time, keep balances manageable, and honor your financial commitments, you build trust. This trust is reflected in your credit history and, in many countries, your credit score.

A strong credit profile can make it easier to qualify for:

- Home mortgages
- Vehicle financing
- Business loans
- Lower interest rates
- Rental agreements
- Certain employment opportunities

Your credit history tells a story. Make sure it is one that reflects responsibility and integrity.

## The Hidden Cost of Debt

Every dollar used to repay unnecessary debt is a dollar that cannot be invested, saved, or used to build wealth.

Imagine paying hundreds of dollars each month in credit card interest.

Now imagine investing that same amount consistently for twenty years.

The difference can be life-changing.

Debt not only costs money—it also costs opportunity.

One of the greatest principles of wealth building is reducing the amount of money working against you and increasing the amount working for you.

## Types of Debt

Not all debt serves the same purpose.

**Productive Debt**

Productive debt is used to acquire assets or improve your future earning potential.

Examples include:

- Purchasing an affordable home
- Investing in education or professional certifications
- Financing a business with a sound plan
- Purchasing equipment that increases income
- Buying an investment property

These decisions should be based on careful planning and realistic repayment strategies.

**Consumer Debt**

Consumer debt is generally used to purchase items that lose value or provide only short-term satisfaction.

Examples include:

- High-interest credit cards
- Luxury purchases
- Impulse shopping
- Financing expensive vacations
- Constant "buy now, pay later" purchases

These forms of debt often delay wealth building because they create ongoing obligations without producing long-term financial value.

## Avoid Lifestyle Inflation

One of the biggest financial traps is increasing your spending every time your income increases.

A promotion leads to a larger car payment.

A salary increase leads to a bigger house.

A bonus leads to expensive purchases.

Soon, higher income simply supports a more expensive lifestyle instead of building greater wealth.

Instead of increasing every expense, consider increasing your investments.

Allow your income to improve your future—not just your lifestyle.

## Building Excellent Credit

Healthy credit habits include:

- Paying every bill on time
- Keeping credit card balances low
- Borrowing only when necessary
- Reviewing your credit reports regularly
- Avoiding unnecessary loan applications
- Maintaining a realistic budget

Excellent credit is earned through consistency, not perfection.

Every responsible financial decision strengthens your reputation over time.

## A Debt Elimination Strategy

If you currently have debt, remember this:

Debt does not define you.

It simply requires a plan.

Start by listing every debt you owe.

Record:

- Total balance
- Interest rate
- Minimum monthly payment
- Remaining repayment period

Then choose a strategy.

Some people prefer paying the smallest balance first to build momentum.

Others focus on paying the highest interest rate first to save money over time.

Whichever approach you choose, remain consistent.

Progress matters more than perfection.

## Borrow for Opportunity, Not for Lifestyle

Before taking on new debt, ask yourself:

- Is this purchase an asset or a liability?
- Will it increase my income or improve my long-term financial position?
- Can I comfortably repay this debt?
- What opportunities might I sacrifice because of these payments?
- Would waiting and saving be the wiser choice?

Thoughtful questions often prevent costly mistakes.

## Financial Freedom Begins with Margin

Imagine living without worrying about monthly loan payments.

Imagine directing money toward investments instead of interest.

Imagine having the flexibility to pursue opportunities because your income is not already committed.

This is the freedom that wise debt management can help create.

Reducing unnecessary debt creates financial margin.

Financial margin creates financial peace.

Financial peace allows you to focus on building wealth instead of merely surviving.

## Your Legacy Is Greater Than Your Liabilities

One day, your children will remember more than the things you purchased.

They will remember the financial example you set.

They will remember whether you planned wisely, lived responsibly, honored your commitments, and made decisions that strengthened your family's future.

Managing debt wisely is not simply about improving your finances today.

It is about creating greater opportunities for tomorrow.

## Legacy Builder Spotlight

**Dave Ramsey: Living Debt-Free**

Financial educator Dave Ramsey has spent decades teaching families how to eliminate debt, live below their means, and build financial security through disciplined budgeting and consistent saving. While different financial experts may recommend different approaches, Ramsey's central message has helped millions of people regain control of their finances.

His work reminds us of a timeless truth:

**Financial peace is often built one disciplined decision at a time.**

## Generational Wealth Principle

"Every dollar spent paying unnecessary interest is a dollar that cannot build your family's future."

## Wealth Reflection

Debt should never become a permanent companion on your financial journey. When used wisely, credit can open doors. When misused, it can quietly close opportunities. The goal is not simply to owe less—it is to create more freedom for yourself and for the generations that follow.

---

## Action Steps

☐ List every outstanding debt you currently owe.

☐ Identify the interest rate on each debt.

☐ Choose a debt repayment strategy and commit to it.

☐ Review your credit history or credit report if available.

☐ Delay one unnecessary purchase this month and redirect that money toward debt reduction or savings.

---

## ⍰ Coach's Corner

Many people feel ashamed of debt, but shame has never solved a financial problem. Knowledge, discipline, and consistent action do. Wherever you are today, remember that every payment you make is one step closer to greater freedom. Focus on progress, celebrate small victories, and keep moving forward. The habits you develop now will benefit not only you but also the generations who follow.

---

## Planner Connection

In your Generational Wealth Planner, complete the Debt Inventory Worksheet, Debt Payoff Strategy, Credit Improvement Checklist, Monthly Debt Tracker, and Debt-Free Milestone Planner. These tools will help you monitor your progress and stay motivated as you work toward financial freedom.

# Chapter Seven

# Building Assets: Making Your Money Work for You

## "The wealth of the wise is their crown..."

## — Proverbs 14:24 (NIV)

## The Difference Between Working for Money and Having Money Work for You

Most people spend their lives working for money. They wake up each morning, go to work, receive a paycheck, pay their bills, and begin the cycle again. There is nothing wrong with working hard. Honest work is honorable and provides for our families. However, if your income stops the moment you stop working, your financial future depends entirely on your ability to continue earning.

Generational wealth requires a different approach. It requires learning how to make your money work for you. This happens through assets. Assets have the potential to grow in value, produce income, or both. While you sleep, travel, spend time with your family, or enjoy retirement, well-chosen assets can continue generating wealth.

The goal is not simply to earn more money. The goal is to own things that continue producing value long after they have been acquired.

## What Is an Asset?

An asset is anything you own that has the potential to increase your financial strength. Some assets appreciate in value over time. Others generate regular income. The strongest financial plans often include a combination of both.

Examples of assets include:

- Your home (depending on how it is used and financed)
- Rental properties
- Stocks and shares
- Mutual funds and exchange-traded funds (ETFs)
- Bonds
- Retirement accounts
- Businesses
- Precious metals
- Agricultural land
- Intellectual property
- Royalties from books, music, or digital products
- Patents and trademarks

Each of these assets has different levels of risk and potential reward, but they all share one important characteristic:

They can create value beyond your paycheck.

## Assets vs. Liabilities

One of the most important financial lessons is learning to distinguish between assets and liabilities.

An **asset** generally puts money into your pocket or increases your overall financial position.

A **liability** usually takes money out of your pocket through ongoing expenses or declining value.

For example:

An investment property that generates rental income is typically an asset.

A luxury vehicle that rapidly depreciates while requiring loan payments, insurance, and maintenance is generally a liability.

Before making a major purchase, ask yourself:

**"Will this purchase strengthen my financial future or simply increase my monthly expenses?"**

That one question can prevent many costly mistakes.

## Real Estate: Building Wealth Through Property

Real estate has helped countless families create long-term wealth.

Property can appreciate over time, generate rental income, and provide financial stability.

Examples include:

- A primary residence
- Rental apartments
- Vacation rentals
- Commercial property
- Agricultural land

However, not every property purchase is automatically a good investment.

Location, financing, maintenance costs, and long-term demand all matter.

Wise investors research thoroughly before making significant property decisions.

## Investing in the Stock Market

Owning shares in successful companies allows ordinary people to participate in the growth of businesses around the world.

Historically, diversified stock market investments have produced long-term growth, although values rise and fall over time.

For beginners, investing through diversified mutual funds or exchange-traded funds (ETFs) can reduce risk by spreading investments across many companies.

Investing is not gambling.

It is becoming a partial owner in businesses that create value over time.

The key is patience, consistency, and a long-term perspective.

## Businesses: An Asset That Can Outlive You

A well-managed business can become one of the greatest sources of generational wealth.

Businesses create jobs.

They solve problems.

They generate income.

They can often be sold, expanded, or passed to future generations.

Many of the world's wealthiest families built their fortunes through business ownership.

Whether you own a neighborhood bakery, an accounting firm, a consulting practice, or an online business, entrepreneurship can create opportunities far beyond a traditional salary.

## Intellectual Property: Wealth Created from Ideas

One of the most overlooked assets is intellectual property.

Books. Courses. Music. Software. Photography. Educational materials. Patents. Digital templates.

These creations can continue producing income for years after the initial work has been completed.

Unlike many physical assets, intellectual property can often be sold repeatedly without being replaced.

For authors, educators, artists, and entrepreneurs, ideas themselves can become valuable financial assets.

## Precious Metals and Alternative Assets

Many investors choose to diversify their wealth by holding assets such as gold and silver.

These precious metals have historically been used as stores of value during periods of economic uncertainty.

Other alternative assets may include collectibles, fine art, or agricultural investments.

While these can play a role in a diversified portfolio, they should generally complement—not replace—a balanced investment strategy.

Diversification helps reduce risk by avoiding dependence on any single asset class.

## The Power of Compound Growth

One of the greatest advantages of investing is compound growth.

When investments generate returns and those returns are reinvested, your money begins earning money on the money it has already earned.

Over time, this creates exponential growth.

The earlier you begin, the greater the potential impact.

Compound growth rewards patience.

It reminds us that wealth is often built gradually rather than instantly.

## Diversification: Don't Put All Your Eggs in One Basket

One of the oldest investment principles remains one of the wisest.

Avoid placing all your resources into a single investment.

Instead, diversify.

Diversification means spreading your investments across different types of assets.

For example:

- Real estate
- Stocks
- Retirement accounts
- Precious metals
- Businesses
- Cash reserves

Diversification helps protect your wealth if one investment performs poorly.

It is a strategy of wisdom, not fear.

## Building Your Asset Portfolio

Building wealth does not happen overnight.

It happens one asset at a time.

Perhaps your first asset is an emergency fund.

Then a retirement account.

Later, a home.

Eventually, investments, business ownership, or rental property.

The important thing is to begin.

Every asset you acquire has the potential to strengthen your family's future and create opportunities for generations to come.

## Think Beyond Your Lifetime

The purpose of building assets is not merely to increase your net worth.

It is to create opportunities. Imagine your children inheriting income-producing property.

Imagine your grandchildren benefiting from investment accounts established decades earlier.

Imagine your family continuing to receive royalties from books, music, educational programs, or businesses long after you are gone.

This is the true power of assets. They can continue working across generations. That is why asset ownership sits at the very heart of generational wealth.

---

## Legacy Builder Spotlight

**Madam C. J. Walker: Building Wealth Through Entrepreneurship**

Madam C. J. Walker transformed a personal challenge into a thriving business by creating hair-care products that met the needs of Black women in the early twentieth century. Through innovation, determination, and business ownership, she became one of America's first self-made female millionaires.

Her success was not built on luck. It was built on solving a problem, creating value, and owning the business she developed.

Her story reminds us that wealth often begins with serving others and having the courage to build something of your own.

---

## Wealth in Action

James and Alana spent years saving money in a regular bank account but saw very little growth. After learning about investing, they decided to keep their emergency fund in savings while gradually investing a portion of their monthly income into a diversified investment fund.

A few years later, they purchased a small rental property that generated additional monthly income. Instead of spending that extra income, they used it to invest further and eventually help pay for their daughter's university education.

Their financial future changed not because they earned extraordinary salaries, but because they began converting savings into assets.

## Generational Wealth Principle

**"Income pays today's bills. Assets pay tomorrow's opportunities."**

## Wealth Reflection

Assets are more than possessions—they are tools that can generate income, appreciate in value, and create opportunities for future generations. Every asset you build today has the potential to become part of your family's legacy tomorrow.

## Action Steps

☐ List all the assets you currently own.

☐ Identify one new asset you would like to acquire within the next five years.

☐ Research one investment option that matches your financial goals and risk tolerance.

☐ Begin setting aside money specifically for purchasing an income-producing asset.

☐ Discuss with your family how asset ownership can strengthen your long-term financial future.

---

## ◈ Coach's Corner

One of the biggest shifts in building generational wealth is moving from a consumer mindset to an ownership mindset. Consumers ask, "What can I buy?" Wealth builders ask, "What can I own that will continue creating value?" Every asset you acquire becomes another employee working on behalf of your family's future. Start small if necessary, but never stop building.

---

## Planner Connection

In your Generational Wealth Planner, complete the Asset Inventory, Net Worth Tracker, Investment Goals Worksheet, Asset Acquisition Plan, and Five-Year Wealth Roadmap. These tools will help you identify where you are today and create a practical strategy for steadily building income-producing assets.

# Chapter Eight

## Multiple Streams of Income: Creating Financial Stability and Freedom

**"Give portions to seven, yes to eight, for you do not know what disaster may come upon the land."**

**— Ecclesiastes 11:2 (NIV)**

### Why One Income Is No Longer Enough

For generations, many people believed that obtaining a stable job and working faithfully until retirement was the safest path to financial security.

While employment remains an important source of income, today's economy has shown us that relying on a single paycheck can leave families vulnerable. Companies restructure, industries evolve, unexpected illnesses occur, and economic conditions change.

When one source of income disappears, the financial impact can be immediate.

Generational wealth requires a different mindset.

Rather than relying on one source of income, wealth builders seek to create multiple streams of income that work together to provide stability, flexibility, and long-term growth.

Think of it this way.

If one stream slows down, the others continue flowing.

That is the strength of diversification.

---

## Biblical Wisdom

**"Give portions to seven, yes to eight, for you do not know what disaster may come upon the land."**

**— Ecclesiastes 11:2 (NIV)**

King Solomon reminds us that wisdom prepares for uncertainty. During his time, families depended on agriculture, livestock, and trade for survival. A drought, storm, disease, or failed harvest could wipe out an entire year's income. Rather than placing all their hope in one source of provision, Solomon encouraged people to spread their resources wisely.

Today, this timeless principle can be applied through diversification. Instead of depending solely on one paycheck, we can strengthen our financial future by developing multiple streams of income, maintaining an emergency fund, investing across different types of assets, and continually developing new skills.

This verse is not encouraging fear of the future—it is encouraging **wise stewardship**. We cannot predict every challenge life will bring, but we can prepare responsibly while trusting God to guide and provide.

**Biblical Principle:** *Preparation is an act of wisdom, and diversification is one way we faithfully steward the resources God has entrusted to us.*

---

## The Difference Between Income and Wealth

Income is what you earn.

Wealth is what you keep, grow, and multiply.

Multiple income streams help bridge that gap.

Instead of depending entirely on one employer, you gradually develop additional sources that strengthen your financial position and reduce risk.

Each new income stream becomes another pillar supporting your family's financial future.

## The Seven Types of Income

Financial educators often describe several categories of income. Understanding them helps you identify opportunities that align with your goals and skills.

**1. Earned Income**

This is the income most people know best.

Examples include:

- Salary
- Wages
- Bonuses
- Overtime
- Professional fees

Earned income is valuable because it often provides the capital needed to build other income streams.

**2. Business Income**

Business income comes from owning a business rather than simply working for someone else.

Examples include:

- Retail stores
- Consulting businesses
- Service companies
- Online businesses
- Coaching

- Freelancing

A successful business has the potential to grow beyond the owner's personal working hours.

**3. Investment Income**

Investment income is generated by money that has been invested.

Examples include:

- Stocks
- Bonds
- Mutual funds
- Exchange-traded funds (ETFs)
- Interest-bearing accounts

Over time, investments allow your money to begin working for you.

**4. Rental Income**

Property ownership can create consistent monthly cash flow through rental payments.

Examples include:

- Residential homes
- Apartments
- Commercial buildings
- Vacation rentals

Rental income has helped countless families build long-term wealth while increasing their net worth through property appreciation.

**5. Royalty Income**

Royalties are earned when creative or intellectual work continues generating revenue after it has been created.

Examples include:

- Books
- Music
- Educational courses
- Software
- Photography
- Patents
- Licensing agreements

One of the greatest advantages of royalty income is that the work can continue producing revenue long after it has been completed.

**6. Dividend Income**

Some companies share a portion of their profits with shareholders through dividend payments.

These regular payments can provide an additional source of income while allowing investments to continue growing.

**7. Digital Income**

Technology has created opportunities that previous generations could scarcely imagine.

Examples include:

- Online courses
- Membership communities
- Digital templates
- Printable planners
- Mobile applications
- Subscription services
- E-books
- Educational resources

Digital products can often be created once and sold many times, making them attractive long-term assets.

## Start with What You Already Know

One of the biggest misconceptions about creating additional income is believing that you must invent something completely new.

In reality, many successful businesses begin with existing knowledge or skills.

Ask yourself:

- What problems can I solve?
- What skills have I developed through my career?
- What knowledge do people regularly ask me to share?
- What hobbies could become a business?
- What experiences could help someone else?

Often, your next income stream is hidden within the skills you already possess.

## Don't Build Everything at Once

A common mistake is trying to launch several businesses or investments simultaneously.

Generational wealth is built patiently.

Start with one additional income stream.

Learn it. Strengthen it. Allow it to become stable.

Then consider adding another.

Consistency almost always outperforms constant distraction.

## Turn Income into Assets

As your additional income grows, resist the temptation to immediately increase your lifestyle.

Instead, ask yourself:

Can this income purchase an appreciating asset?

Can it reduce debt?

Can it increase my investments?

Can it help fund another income-producing opportunity?

The purpose of additional income is not merely to spend more.

Its purpose is to create even greater financial opportunities.

## Create Income That Can Outlive You

One of the greatest characteristics of generational wealth is creating income that continues beyond your lifetime.

A family business may continue serving customers.

Investment portfolios may continue growing.

Rental properties may continue producing income.

Books may continue selling.

Educational courses may continue enrolling students.

Royalties may continue being paid.

Businesses may continue expanding.

The goal is not simply to earn income while you are alive.

The goal is to create assets that continue blessing future generations.

## Protect Your Time

While creating multiple streams of income is important, remember that wealth should improve your life—not consume it.

Avoid becoming so busy pursuing money that you neglect your health, relationships, faith, or personal well-being.

True wealth includes balance.

The greatest legacy you leave your family is not only financial security but also your presence, wisdom, and example.

## Build One Stream at a Time

You do not need seven income streams tomorrow.

You need one additional stream that is built with excellence.

Then another.

Then another.

Over time, those streams become a river.

A river that provides stability.

Opportunity.

Freedom.

And eventually, a lasting legacy for generations to come.

---

## Legacy Builder Spotlight

**Walt Disney: Turning Creativity into Generational Wealth**

Walt Disney began with a simple talent for storytelling. Through persistence, innovation, and entrepreneurship, he transformed that talent into books, films, merchandise, theme parks, licensing agreements, and one of the world's most recognizable brands.

His legacy demonstrates that an idea, when developed with vision and excellence, can grow into multiple streams of income that continue creating value for generations.

His story reminds us that creativity is not merely artistic—it can also become a powerful financial asset.

## Wealth in Action

Angela worked full-time as a teacher. Rather than relying solely on her salary, she began tutoring students in the evenings. Later, she created digital study guides and online lessons that she sold throughout the year.

The extra income helped her eliminate debt, build an emergency fund, and invest consistently. Within a few years, she was earning money from several different sources instead of depending on one paycheck.

She did not become financially secure overnight.

She became financially stronger one income stream at a time.

## Generational Wealth Principle

**"A single paycheck can support today, but multiple streams of income help secure tomorrow."**

## Wealth Reflection

Multiple streams of income provide more than financial security—they provide flexibility, resilience, and opportunity. As each stream grows, so does your ability to invest, give generously, weather financial challenges, and build a legacy that extends beyond your lifetime.

## Action Steps

☐ List every source of income you currently have.

☐ Identify one skill or area of knowledge that could generate additional income.

☐ Research one business, investment, or digital opportunity that aligns with your interests.

☐Create a six-month plan for developing one new income stream.

☐ Decide how you will use any additional income to strengthen your family's long-term financial position.

---

## ◈ Coach's Corner

Don't become discouraged if your first additional income stream generates only a modest amount. Every successful business, investment portfolio, and royalty stream began somewhere. Focus on excellence, consistency, and continual improvement. Remember, the goal is not to become busy with countless projects—the goal is to build reliable streams of income that steadily strengthen your family's financial future.

---

## Planner Connection

In your Generational Wealth Planner, complete the Income Streams Assessment, Side Business Brainstorm Worksheet, Business Start-Up Planner, Passive Income Tracker, Income Diversification Roadmap, and Five-Year Income Growth Plan. These exercises will help you identify opportunities to increase your earning potential while creating long-term financial stability.

# Chapter Nine

# Protecting Your Legacy: Insurance, Wills, and Estate Planning

## "The prudent see danger and take refuge, but the simple keep going and pay the penalty."

## — Proverbs 22:3 (NIV)

## Building Wealth Is Only Half the Journey

Many people spend years working hard to earn money, purchase a home, build a business, invest for the future, and provide for their families.

Yet one unexpected event—a serious illness, a disability, a natural disaster, a lawsuit, or an untimely death—can place everything they have worked so hard to build at risk.

Generational wealth is not created simply by accumulating assets.

It is preserved by protecting them.

Protection is one of the most overlooked principles of financial success. Wealth builders understand that preparing for uncertainty is not pessimism—it is wisdom.

Insurance, wills, and estate planning are not conversations we should avoid. They are acts of love, responsibility, and foresight.

---

## Biblical Wisdom

**"The prudent see danger and take refuge, but the simple keep going and pay the penalty."**

**— Proverbs 22:3 (NIV)**

Throughout the book of Proverbs, wisdom is often described as the ability to anticipate future consequences and act before problems arise. This verse teaches that a prudent person does not ignore potential risks—they prepare for them.

In today's world, that preparation may include purchasing adequate insurance, creating a will, organizing important legal documents, establishing an estate plan, and ensuring that loved ones are protected if unexpected circumstances arise.

Some people avoid these conversations because they believe planning for illness, disability, or death reflects a lack of faith. Scripture presents a different perspective. Biblical wisdom encourages us to be both faithful and prepared. Noah built the ark before the flood came. Joseph stored grain before the famine arrived. Likewise, protecting our families through thoughtful financial planning is an act of responsible stewardship.

Planning ahead is not rooted in fear.

It is rooted in wisdom, love, and responsibility.

**Biblical Principle:** *Faith trusts God, while wisdom prepares for life's uncertainties.*

---

## Why Protection Matters

Imagine spending thirty years building a successful business without having business insurance.

Imagine purchasing a family home without homeowners insurance.

Imagine raising children without life insurance to provide for them if something unexpected happened.

Imagine passing away without leaving instructions for how your assets should be distributed.

Each of these situations could create unnecessary financial hardship for the people you love most.

Planning ahead protects your family from confusion, financial stress, and avoidable legal challenges.

## Understanding Insurance

Insurance is a financial safety net.

It allows many people to contribute small amounts of money through premiums so that those who experience unexpected losses receive financial support.

While paying insurance premiums may sometimes feel like an expense you hope never to use, the true value of insurance lies in the protection it provides when life takes an unexpected turn.

Insurance does not prevent difficult situations.

It helps reduce their financial impact.

## Types of Insurance Everyone Should Consider

While every family has different needs, understanding the most common forms of insurance can help you make informed decisions.

**Health Insurance**

Medical emergencies can happen without warning.

Health insurance helps reduce the financial burden of medical treatment, hospital stays, surgeries, and ongoing healthcare.

Protecting your health also protects your finances.

**Life Insurance**

Life insurance provides financial support to the people who depend on you after your death.

It can help cover:

- Daily living expenses
- Mortgage payments
- Children's education
- Funeral expenses
- Outstanding debts
- Family income replacement

For many families, life insurance is one of the most important tools for protecting generational wealth.

**Homeowners or Property Insurance**

For many families, their home is one of their largest financial assets.

Property insurance helps protect against losses caused by events such as fire, storms, theft, or other covered damages.

Without adequate coverage, rebuilding after a disaster could become financially overwhelming.

**Vehicle Insurance**

Automobile accidents can result in significant repair costs, medical expenses, or legal claims.

Appropriate vehicle insurance helps reduce these financial risks while providing peace of mind.

### Disability Insurance

Many people insure their homes and vehicles but overlook one of their greatest financial assets—their ability to earn an income.

Disability insurance helps replace a portion of your income if illness or injury prevents you from working.

For individuals whose families depend on their income, this protection can be invaluable.

### Business Insurance

Entrepreneurs invest significant time, money, and energy into building their businesses.

Business insurance can help protect against property damage, legal liability, interruptions to operations, and other risks that could threaten years of hard work.

## What Is a Will?

A will is a legal document that communicates your wishes regarding the distribution of your assets after your death.

Without a valid will, decisions about your estate may be made according to the laws of your country or state rather than your personal wishes.

A will allows you to:

- Name beneficiaries.
- Appoint guardians for minor children.
- Identify an executor to manage your estate.
- Reduce confusion among family members.
- Help minimize unnecessary legal disputes.

Creating a will is not reserved for the wealthy.

Anyone who owns property, has savings, operates a business, or has children should consider preparing one.

## Understanding Estate Planning

Many people believe estate planning is only for millionaires.

In reality, estate planning is simply the process of organizing your financial affairs so that your assets can be transferred smoothly and according to your wishes.

Estate planning may include:

- Wills
- Trusts
- Powers of attorney
- Healthcare directives
- Beneficiary designations
- Business succession plans
- Tax planning strategies

The purpose is not merely to distribute wealth.

The purpose is to preserve your legacy while reducing unnecessary stress for your family.

## Keep Your Documents Updated

Life changes. Marriage. Divorce. Birth of children. Purchase of property. Starting a business. Retirement.

Because of these changes, important legal and financial documents should be reviewed regularly.

An outdated will or insurance policy may no longer reflect your wishes or adequately protect your family.

Reviewing these documents every few years—or after major life events—is a wise habit.

## Protection Is an Act of Love

Some people avoid discussing wills because they believe doing so invites misfortune.

Others delay purchasing insurance because they prefer not to think about worst-case scenarios.

In reality, planning ahead demonstrates love and responsibility.

When you organize your affairs, you spare your family unnecessary confusion during what may already be one of the most difficult seasons of their lives.

Preparing today is one of the greatest gifts you can give tomorrow.

## Think Beyond Yourself

Generational wealth is not simply about what you accumulate while you are alive.

It is about what continues after you are gone.

Ask yourself:

- Would my family know where my important documents are located?
- Do my loved ones understand my financial wishes?
- Have I named beneficiaries on my accounts?
- Would my children be financially protected?
- Have I prepared my business to continue if something happened to me?

These questions are not signs of fear.

They are signs of wisdom.

## Legacy Is Protected Through Preparation

Building wealth requires discipline.

Protecting wealth requires planning.

Passing wealth to future generations requires intentional action.

The strongest financial legacies are not left to chance.

They are carefully prepared.

Insurance protects your family.

A will protects your wishes.

Estate planning protects your legacy.

Together, they become some of the most powerful acts of financial stewardship you can make.

---

## Legacy Builder Spotlight

**Andrew Carnegie: Planning Beyond a Lifetime**

Andrew Carnegie built one of the largest fortunes of his era through the steel industry. Yet his enduring legacy is not measured only by the wealth he accumulated, but by how intentionally he planned for it to benefit others.

During his lifetime, Carnegie funded thousands of public libraries, educational institutions, and charitable initiatives that continue serving communities today.

His example reminds us that the greatest measure of wealth is not only what we leave behind, but how thoughtfully we prepare it to serve future generations.

---

## Wealth in Action

Michael and Denise spent years building their savings, purchasing a family home, and growing a small business. After attending a financial planning seminar, they realized they had no will, no updated beneficiaries, and inadequate life insurance.

Over the next few months, they met with qualified professionals to prepare a will, increase their insurance coverage, organize important documents, and create an estate plan.

They didn't become wealthier overnight—but they became significantly more secure.

Their children now have greater protection because their parents chose to prepare instead of postpone.

## Generational Wealth Principle

**"Building wealth creates opportunity. Protecting wealth preserves opportunity for generations."**

## Wealth Reflection

Preparing for life's uncertainties is not about expecting the worst—it is about loving your family enough to plan wisely. Insurance, wills, and estate planning provide peace of mind today while protecting the people and assets you value most tomorrow.

## Action Steps

☐ Review all of your current insurance policies.

☐ Make a list of your beneficiaries and confirm they are up to date.

☐ Create or review your will with a qualified legal professional.

☐ Organize important financial documents in a secure location.

☐ Discuss your estate wishes with trusted family members when appropriate.

---

## ◈ Coach's Corner

Many people postpone estate planning because they believe they have plenty of time. Unfortunately, life does not always follow our schedules. Preparing today is one of the greatest demonstrations of love and responsibility you can show your family. The conversations may feel uncomfortable, but the peace of mind they provide is invaluable.

## Planner Connection

In your Generational Wealth Planner, complete the Insurance Review Checklist, Estate Planning Organizer, Beneficiary Record, Important Documents Inventory, Family Emergency Information Sheet, and Legacy Protection Checklist. These resources will help you organize your financial affairs and ensure that your plans remain current as your life evolves.

# PART III – Protecting Wealth

# Chapter Ten

# Retirement Planning: Securing Your Future While Protecting Your Legacy

## "The plans of the diligent lead surely to abundance, but everyone who is hasty comes only to poverty."

## — Proverbs 21:5 (ESV)

## Retirement Is Not the End—It Is a New Beginning

For many people, retirement represents the reward for decades of hard work. It is a season to enjoy family, pursue personal interests, serve the community, travel, and experience the fruit of years of faithful planning.

Unfortunately, many people reach retirement unprepared.

Some depend entirely on government pensions.

Others rely solely on their children.

Many discover too late that they have not saved enough to maintain the lifestyle they hoped to enjoy.

Generational wealth requires us to think differently.

Retirement planning is not only about providing for ourselves—it is about ensuring that our later years do not become a financial burden on those we love while preserving the wealth we have worked so hard to build.

## Biblical Wisdom

**"The plans of the diligent lead surely to abundance, but everyone who is hasty comes only to poverty."**

**— Proverbs 21:5 (ESV)**

Scripture repeatedly teaches the value of thoughtful planning. God calls us to be diligent, faithful stewards who prepare wisely rather than living only for today.

Retirement planning reflects this principle. Setting aside money consistently, investing wisely, reducing unnecessary debt, and preparing for future needs are practical expressions of diligence.

Planning for retirement is not about fearing old age.

It is about honoring God through wise stewardship, caring responsibly for yourself, and preserving your family's financial stability.

**Biblical Principle:** *Wise planning today creates greater freedom tomorrow.*

## Why Retirement Planning Matters

Retirement planning provides more than financial security.

It provides choices.

It allows you to decide how you will spend your later years rather than allowing financial limitations to make those decisions for you.

With thoughtful preparation, retirement can become a season to:

- Spend more time with family.
- Mentor younger generations.
- Volunteer or serve your community.
- Pursue lifelong interests.
- Travel.

- Continue managing businesses or investments.
- Support charitable causes.

Financial preparation creates flexibility.

## Start Planning Early

One of the greatest advantages in retirement planning is time.

The earlier you begin saving and investing, the more opportunity your money has to grow through compound returns.

Many people believe they must save large amounts to make a difference.

The truth is that consistency often matters more than the starting amount.

A small contribution made regularly over many years can grow into significant financial resources.

The best time to begin was yesterday.

The second-best time is today.

## Understand Your Retirement Income

Retirement income may come from several different sources.

These may include:

- Government pension or social security benefits.
- Employer-sponsored retirement plans.
- Personal retirement accounts.
- Investment portfolios.
- Rental properties.
- Business income.
- Royalties.
- Dividend income.

- Personal savings.

The more diversified your retirement income, the greater your financial resilience.

## Estimate Your Retirement Needs

One common mistake is assuming that retirement expenses will automatically decrease.

While some expenses may decline, others often increase.

Healthcare costs.

Home maintenance.

Travel.

Inflation.

Family support.

A realistic retirement plan considers both present and future financial needs.

Ask yourself:

- What lifestyle do I hope to enjoy?
- Where do I plan to live?
- What healthcare needs might I face?
- What income will I need each month?

Answering these questions today helps prevent difficult surprises tomorrow.

## Protect Your Retirement Savings

Building retirement savings requires years of discipline.

Protecting those savings requires wisdom.

Avoid unnecessary withdrawals.

Continue reviewing your investment strategy.

Maintain adequate insurance.

Update your estate plan.

Review beneficiary designations regularly.

Retirement planning is not a one-time event.

It is an ongoing process.

## Retirement and Purpose

One of the greatest misconceptions about retirement is that life loses purpose once full-time employment ends.

Nothing could be further from the truth.

Many retirees discover new opportunities to mentor, teach, volunteer, write, consult, start businesses, or support causes they care deeply about.

Retirement should not simply be about stopping work.

It should be about gaining greater freedom to invest your time in what matters most.

Purpose gives retirement meaning.

## Continue Building Generational Wealth

Retirement does not end your role as a wealth builder.

Many individuals continue investing, mentoring family members, managing businesses, writing books, or creating charitable foundations throughout retirement.

Some of the greatest contributions to future generations are made during this season of life.

Retirement is not merely about preserving wealth.

It is also about transferring wisdom.

Your financial experience may become one of the greatest gifts you ever leave behind.

## Prepare for More Than Yourself

Generational wealth asks a different question.

Not simply:

*"Will I have enough?"*

But also:

*"How can my planning continue benefiting my family long after I am gone?"*

That perspective changes everything.

Retirement planning becomes more than personal security.

It becomes another chapter in building a lasting legacy.

---

## Legacy Builder Spotlight

**Warren Buffett: Long-Term Thinking**

Warren Buffett has consistently emphasized the importance of patience, long-term investing, and allowing compound growth to work over decades rather than seeking quick financial gains.

His investment philosophy demonstrates that wealth is often built through disciplined decisions repeated consistently over a lifetime.

His example reminds us that retirement planning is less about timing the market and more about remaining faithful to a well-designed long-term strategy.

## Wealth in Action

Carlos began contributing a small amount to his retirement account in his twenties. As his income increased, he gradually increased his contributions instead of dramatically increasing his lifestyle.

Years later, he entered retirement with multiple sources of income, including a pension, investment portfolio, and rental property.

Because he planned consistently over many years, retirement became a season of freedom rather than financial uncertainty.

**Generational Wealth Principle**

**"Retirement is not the reward for building wealth—it is the season in which wise planning continues to protect it."**

## Wealth Reflection

Retirement planning is an investment in your future independence and your family's long-term stability. Every contribution you make today strengthens your ability to enjoy tomorrow with confidence, dignity, and purpose.

## Action Steps

- ☐ Estimate the monthly income you will need during retirement.
- ☐ Review your current retirement savings and investments.
- ☐ Increase your retirement contribution if your budget allows.

☐ Identify one additional source of retirement income you would like to develop.

☐ Schedule an annual retirement planning review.

---

## ◈ Coach's Corner

Many people postpone retirement planning because retirement seems far away. The truth is that time is one of your greatest financial allies. Even small, consistent contributions made over many years can produce remarkable results. Don't focus on where you wish you had started. Focus on taking the next wise step today. Your future self will thank you for it.

---

## Questions to Discuss with a Financial Professional

- Am I saving enough to meet my retirement goals?
- Which retirement accounts are available in my country or through my employer?
- Is my investment portfolio appropriate for my age and risk tolerance?
- How should I prepare for healthcare expenses in retirement?
- How can I generate reliable retirement income while preserving my assets for future generations?

---

## Planner Connection

In your Generational Wealth Planner, complete the Retirement Vision Worksheet, Retirement Savings Tracker, Future Income Calculator, Retirement Expense Planner, Annual Retirement Review Checklist, and Legacy Income Plan. These tools will help you create a practical roadmap toward financial independence while preserving your family's long-term wealth.

# Chapter Eleven

# Teaching the Next Generation About Money

## "Train up a child in the way he should go, and when he is old he will not depart from it."

## — Proverbs 22:6 (NKJV)

## Wealth Is More Than an Inheritance

When most people hear the word **inheritance**, they immediately think about money, property, investments, or valuable possessions.

While these gifts can certainly improve a person's financial future, they are not the greatest inheritance a parent can leave.

Imagine inheriting a million dollars without knowing how to budget, invest, or manage debt.

How long would that wealth last?

History has shown that wealth alone is rarely enough. Without wisdom, discipline, and character, even large fortunes can disappear within a generation.

The greatest inheritance you can leave your children is not simply financial wealth—it is financial wisdom.

When knowledge accompanies wealth, the next generation is better prepared to protect, grow, and multiply what has been entrusted to them.

## Children Learn More from What They See Than What They Hear

Parents often spend years telling their children to save money, avoid debt, and make wise financial decisions.

But children learn far more from observation than instruction.

They watch how we spend.

They notice how we react to financial stress.

They observe whether we budget, save, give generously, or make impulsive purchases.

Our daily habits become their first financial education.

If they regularly witness responsible financial behavior, those habits are more likely to become part of their own lives.

The greatest financial lessons are often taught without saying a word.

## Start Teaching Early

Financial education should not begin when children become adults.

It should begin as early as they are able to understand basic concepts.

Young children can learn:

- The difference between needs and wants.
- Why we save money.
- Why we should not spend everything we receive.
- The joy of giving.
- The importance of gratitude.

As children mature, their financial education should grow with them.

Teenagers can begin learning about:

- Budgeting.
- Banking.

- Credit.
- Investing.
- Entrepreneurship.
- Taxes.
- Insurance.
- Retirement planning.

By adulthood, financial conversations should feel natural rather than unfamiliar.

## Teach Through Everyday Experiences

Some of the best financial lessons happen during ordinary moments.

Take your children grocery shopping.

Show them how to compare prices.

Explain why you choose one product over another.

Allow them to help create a family budget.

Discuss saving for family goals.

Include them in age-appropriate financial decisions.

Money should not become a forbidden topic.

It should become an ongoing family conversation.

## Teach the Difference Between Wealth and Lifestyle

Many young people grow up believing that expensive possessions indicate financial success.

Social media often reinforces this message.

Luxury vehicles.

Designer clothing.

Exotic vacations.

Large homes.

These images tell only part of the story.

Teach your children that appearances can be misleading.

Real wealth is often quiet.

It is found in responsible planning, consistent investing, disciplined saving, wise decision-making, and ownership of appreciating assets.

A wealthy lifestyle and a wealthy balance sheet are not always the same thing.

Help them understand the difference.

## Encourage Entrepreneurship

Employment is valuable.

Entrepreneurship creates additional opportunities.

Encourage your children to explore their talents.

Support their ideas.

Celebrate creativity.

Whether they start a lawn care business, sell handmade products, tutor students, create digital products, or launch an online business, entrepreneurship teaches valuable lessons about responsibility, problem-solving, customer service, and perseverance.

Even if their first business is small, the experience can shape their confidence for a lifetime.

## Talk About Mistakes

One of the greatest gifts parents can give their children is honesty.

Share lessons from your own financial journey.

Discuss mistakes you made.

Explain what you learned.

Describe how you recovered.

Children do not need parents who are perfect.

They need parents who are willing to teach with humility.

Your experience can help them avoid repeating the same mistakes.

## Teach Generosity Alongside Wealth

Money should never become the ultimate goal.

Teach your children that wealth carries responsibility.

Encourage generosity.

Support charitable causes together.

Volunteer as a family.

Help others in need.

When children learn that money can be used to bless others, they develop a healthier relationship with wealth.

Generosity protects the heart from greed.

It reminds us that true wealth is measured not only by what we keep but also by what we contribute.

## Create Family Financial Traditions

Every family has traditions.

Some celebrate holidays.

Others gather for birthdays or reunions.

Consider creating financial traditions as well.

Examples include:

- Annual family goal-setting meetings.
- Year-end financial reviews.
- Savings challenges.
- Investment education nights.
- Entrepreneur fairs where children present business ideas.
- Family discussions about charitable giving.
- Reading books about money together.

These traditions strengthen both financial literacy and family unity.

## Teach Stewardship, Not Entitlement

One of the greatest dangers of inheritance is entitlement.

Children who receive wealth without understanding responsibility may view money as something to consume rather than something to manage.

Teach them that wealth is a trust.

It carries responsibility.

Every dollar should be managed wisely.

Every opportunity should be appreciated.

Every blessing should be stewarded with gratitude.

Stewardship produces maturity.

Entitlement often destroys it.

## Leave Wisdom Before Wealth

Long before your children inherit your assets, allow them to inherit your wisdom.

Teach them:

- How to earn
- How to save
- How to invest
- How to give
- How to recover from mistakes
- How to make wise decisions
- How to honor God through faithful stewardship

If they receive these lessons, they will possess something that no economic downturn can ever take away.

Knowledge becomes the inheritance that continues paying dividends throughout life.

## Legacy Is a Conversation

Generational wealth is not transferred through a single document.

It is transferred through years of conversations.

Dinner table discussions.

Shared experiences.

Family values.

Consistent examples.

Patient teaching.

Encouraging words.

When financial wisdom becomes part of your family's culture, wealth has a far greater chance of surviving for generations.

Your greatest legacy may not be the money you leave behind.

It may be the wisdom you leave within those you love.

---

◈ **Biblical Wisdom**

**"Train up a child in the way he should go, and when he is old he will not depart from it."**

**— Proverbs 22:6 (NKJV)**

This well-known proverb reminds us that education is one of the greatest investments we can make in the next generation. While it is often applied to spiritual and moral development, its principle also extends to everyday life, including financial stewardship.

Children are not born knowing how to manage money wisely. They learn through instruction, observation, correction, and consistent example. As parents, grandparents, mentors, and caregivers, we have the privilege and responsibility of shaping their understanding of work, generosity, saving, investing, and wise decision-making.

Teaching children about money is not simply preparing them to earn a living—it is preparing them to become faithful stewards of the resources God will one day place in their hands.

**Biblical Principle:** *The greatest financial inheritance begins with intentional teaching.*

---

# Legacy Builder Spotlight

### John D. Rockefeller: Teaching Stewardship at Home

John D. Rockefeller became one of the wealthiest businessmen in history, but he also believed that children should learn responsibility long before they inherited wealth. From an early age, his family emphasized saving, record-keeping, generosity, and disciplined financial habits.

Rockefeller taught that every dollar should have a purpose and encouraged careful stewardship rather than careless spending.

His example reminds us that lasting wealth is built not only through financial success but through intentionally preparing the next generation to manage it wisely.

---

## Wealth in Action

Every Friday evening, Marcus and his wife gathered their children around the kitchen table for what they called "Family Money Night." Together they reviewed savings goals, discussed giving opportunities, and celebrated progress toward family financial goals.

Their children learned how to budget with small allowances, compare prices while shopping, and save for items they wanted instead of expecting instant gratification.

Years later, those lessons became part of the family's culture. Their children entered adulthood with confidence, discipline, and an appreciation for the value of wise financial stewardship.

---

## Generational Wealth Principle

**"The greatest inheritance is not the wealth you leave behind—it is the wisdom you leave within the next generation."**

---

## Wealth Reflection

Financial literacy is not inherited automatically. It is intentionally taught, patiently modeled, and consistently reinforced. Every conversation you have about money today becomes an investment in your family's future tomorrow.

## Action Steps

☐ Schedule your first family financial conversation this month.

☐ Teach your children or grandchildren one new money lesson this week.

☐ Help a child create a simple savings goal.

☐ Share one financial mistake you have learned from and explain the lesson.

☐ Begin creating a written family legacy of financial wisdom to pass on to future generations.

## ⍰ Coach's Corner

Don't wait until your children become adults to talk about money. Some of the most meaningful financial lessons happen during ordinary moments—shopping for groceries, saving for a family vacation, or discussing why you chose to invest instead of spend. These conversations may seem small today, but years from now they could shape the financial future of your children and grandchildren. Remember, every lesson you teach today becomes part of the legacy they carry tomorrow.

## Questions to Discuss as a Family

- What does wealth mean to our family?
- What financial values do we want future generations to remember?
- How can we encourage saving, giving, and investing in age-

appropriate ways?
- What family traditions could help strengthen financial literacy?
- What legacy do we hope our family will leave beyond money?

---

## Planner Connection

In your Generational Wealth Planner, complete the Family Legacy Statement, Children's Financial Education Plan, Family Money Meeting Agenda, Legacy Letter Worksheet, Financial Values Assessment, and Generational Teaching Plan. These tools will help you intentionally pass on both financial knowledge and family values to the next generation.

# Chapter Twelve

# Leaving More Than Money: Building a Legacy That Lasts

## "A good person leaves an inheritance for their children's children..."

## — Proverbs 13:22 (NIV)

## What Will Be Left Behind?

One day, each of us will leave this world.

When that day comes, our possessions will remain:

- Our homes
- Our investments
- Our businesses
- Our savings
- Our personal belongings
- But an even more important question remains:

What will people remember about the life we lived?

Will they remember only the money we accumulated?

Or will they remember the values we demonstrated, the wisdom we shared, the lives we touched, and the opportunities we created for others?

Generational wealth is not measured only by the size of an estate.

It is measured by the strength of a legacy.

## Wealth Is a Tool, Not the Destination

Throughout this book, we have explored budgeting, saving, investing, cash flow, debt management, insurance, retirement planning, asset building, and financial education.

These principles are important.

But they all point toward something greater:

- Money is a tool
- It can educate
- It can heal
- It can provide
- It can create opportunity
- It can build businesses
- It can support ministries
- It can strengthen families

Money itself is never the ultimate goal.

The ultimate goal is using our resources wisely to make a lasting difference.

When wealth has purpose, it becomes legacy.

## The Legacy of Character

There are families who inherit millions of dollars but struggle because honesty, humility, discipline, and responsibility were never taught.

There are also families with modest financial resources whose children become extraordinary leaders because they inherited integrity, perseverance, faith, compassion, and wisdom.

Character outlives possessions.

Teach your children:

- To keep their word.
- To work with excellence.
- To treat others with dignity.
- To live honestly.
- To remain humble.
- To be generous.
- To honor God in every area of life.

These qualities become treasures that no economic downturn can ever remove.

## The Legacy of Education

One of the greatest gifts you can give future generations is a love of learning.

Encourage curiosity.

Read together.

Ask thoughtful questions.

Develop new skills.

Invest in education.

Celebrate lifelong learning.

Knowledge creates opportunities.

Education equips people to solve problems, adapt to change, and continue growing throughout life.

An educated mind is one of the greatest assets a family can possess.

## The Legacy of Service

True wealth is not measured only by what we receive.

It is also measured by what we give.

Some of the most influential people in history are remembered not because they accumulated great wealth, but because they used their resources to improve the lives of others.

Look for opportunities to serve.

Volunteer.

Mentor.

Support charitable causes.

Help someone start a business.

Pay for a student's education.

Encourage a struggling family.

Acts of generosity often create ripple effects that continue for generations.

## The Legacy of Faith

Faith provides a foundation that money alone can never offer.

Financial success may create comfort.

Faith provides hope.

Financial planning prepares us for tomorrow.

Faith gives us courage when tomorrow is uncertain.

Teach future generations to trust God not only during seasons of abundance but also during seasons of difficulty.

When faith and financial wisdom walk together, families develop resilience that extends far beyond material wealth.

## The Legacy of Family

Strong families rarely happen by accident.

They are built intentionally.

Create traditions.

Celebrate milestones.

Share family stories.

Eat meals together.

Pray together.

Encourage one another.

Discuss dreams.

Support each other's goals.

These moments become part of your family's identity.

Years from now, your children may remember conversations around the dinner table more vividly than the gifts they received.

Relationships are part of your inheritance.

## The Legacy of Vision

Every generation should leave the next generation standing on higher ground.

Perhaps your parents gave you determination.

You can add financial wisdom.

Your children can build businesses.

Your grandchildren may establish foundations, schools, or organizations that bless entire communities.

Each generation should build upon the work of the previous one.

That is how legacies grow.

## Your Name Becomes Your Legacy

Long after financial statements have been forgotten, your name will continue to carry meaning.

When future generations hear your name, what do you hope comes to mind?

Integrity?

Generosity?

Leadership?

Faith?

Wisdom?

Compassion?

Courage?

These qualities become part of your family's story.

They are passed from one generation to the next.

They become your true inheritance.

## Becoming the Generation That Changes Everything

Perhaps you were not born into wealth.

Perhaps no one taught you about investing.

Perhaps financial struggle has been part of your family's story for decades.

That does not have to define your future.

Someone must become the generation that chooses a different path.

Someone must decide:

"We will save."

"We will invest."

"We will learn."

"We will build."

"We will protect."

"We will teach."

"We will leave a legacy."

Perhaps that someone is you.

History often remembers the first person who changed the direction of an entire family.

Why shouldn't that person be you?

## The Greatest Investment You Will Ever Make

As you close this book, remember this:

Every budget you create...

Every debt you eliminate...

Every dollar you save...

Every investment you make...

Every business you build...

Every lesson you teach...

Every act of generosity you demonstrate...

Every prayer you pray over your family...

Every conversation you have about money...

Every wise decision you make...

Is another investment in generations you may never meet.

Imagine your great-grandchildren living opportunities that began because of a decision you made today.

Imagine them attending university because you established an education fund.

Imagine them owning a family business because you had the courage to start one.

Imagine them serving others because they watched your example.

That is the true meaning of generational wealth.

It is not about becoming famous.

It is not about becoming the richest person in the room.

It is about becoming the person who changed the future of an entire family.

## Your Legacy Begins Today

The future is not built tomorrow.

It is built today.

With every wise financial decision.

With every lesson you teach.

With every opportunity you create.

With every act of generosity.

With every investment made in faith, wisdom, and love.

No matter where you begin...

No matter what mistakes you have made...

No matter what your current financial situation looks like...

Your legacy is still being written.

May this book inspire you to become a faithful steward, a wise builder, and a courageous visionary.

May your life become a testimony that ordinary people, making extraordinary decisions consistently over time, can change the future of generations.

And may those who come after you rise because you chose to begin.

## ◈ Biblical Wisdom

**"A good person leaves an inheritance for their children's children..."**

**— Proverbs 13:22 (NIV)**

This verse reminds us that God's vision for inheritance extends beyond one generation. While financial resources are certainly included, biblical inheritance also encompasses wisdom, faith, values, integrity, and stewardship.

Leaving an inheritance is not only about what is written in a will. It is about the life you live every day. The conversations you have with your children, the habits you model, the generosity you demonstrate, and the faith you practice become part of the legacy that future generations receive.

The greatest inheritance is one that equips future generations to continue building rather than starting over.

**Biblical Principle:** *A lasting legacy is built through faithful stewardship, intentional teaching, and lives lived with purpose.*

## Legacy Builder Spotlight

**Alfred Nobel: Redefining a Legacy**

Alfred Nobel amassed considerable wealth through his inventions and business ventures. Yet as he reflected on how history might remember him, he made a remarkable decision. Through his will, he established the Nobel Prizes—awards that continue to recognize extraordinary achievements in science, literature, medicine, peace, and economics.

Today, Nobel's name is remembered not primarily for his wealth, but for the enduring impact of the legacy he chose to leave.

His story reminds us that the most meaningful legacy is not measured by what we accumulate, but by the lasting difference we make in the lives of others.

## Wealth in Action

Grace and her husband did not consider themselves wealthy. They worked faithfully, lived within their means, and invested consistently over many years. More importantly, they involved their children in financial conversations, taught them the importance of generosity, encouraged education, and demonstrated integrity in every financial decision.

When they eventually passed on their modest estate, their children inherited more than money—they inherited wisdom, discipline, and values. Those lessons enabled the next generation to build upon the foundation their parents had established.

Their greatest legacy was not their bank account.

It was the family culture they intentionally created.

## Generational Wealth Principle

**"True wealth is measured not only by what you leave behind, but by who your family becomes because you lived."**

## Wealth Reflection

Pause for a moment and imagine your family fifty years from now. What values, opportunities, traditions, and financial foundations do you hope they will inherit because of the choices you are making today? Legacy is not created in a single moment—it is built through a lifetime of faithful decisions.

## Action Steps

☐ Write a one-page Legacy Letter to your family, sharing your values, hopes, and financial lessons.

☐ Create a personal mission statement that will guide your financial decisions.

☐ Identify one family tradition you want to begin this year.

☐ Choose one act of generosity you can practice this month.

☐ Commit to reviewing your legacy plan annually and updating it as your family grows.

## ⯑ Coach's Corner

If you remember only one lesson from this book, let it be this: You do not have to come from a wealthy family to create one. Every generation has the opportunity to make choices that shape the future. You may not control where your story began, but you have tremendous influence over where it goes from here. Build with wisdom. Lead with integrity. Give with generosity. Teach with patience. Love your family well. Years from now, the seeds you plant today may become the harvest your descendants enjoy.

## Questions to Discuss as a Family

- What do we want our family to be known for?
- Which values are non-negotiable in our family?
- How can we use our resources to serve others?
- What traditions should we begin that future generations can continue?
- What kind of legacy do we hope to leave fifty years from now?

---

## Planner Connection

In your Generational Wealth Planner, complete the Legacy Vision Statement, Family Mission Statement, Generational Goals Worksheet, Legacy Letter, Annual Family Legacy Review, and 100-Year Family Vision Plan. These exercises will help transform your hopes into intentional actions that can influence generations to come.

# Final Challenge
# The First Step Begins Today

Congratulations!

By reading this book, you have already done something many people never do—you have chosen to invest in your financial education. Knowledge is one of the greatest assets you will ever acquire because it has the power to transform not only your life but also the lives of generations yet to come.

Throughout these chapters, we have explored what it truly means to build generational wealth. We have discussed the importance of developing the right mindset, cultivating healthy financial habits, mastering cash flow, managing debt wisely, building income-producing assets, creating multiple streams of income, protecting your wealth, planning for retirement, and preparing the next generation to become faithful stewards of what they inherit.

Yet none of these principles will change your life until they become action.

Information inspires.

Action transforms.

One of the greatest mistakes people make after reading a book is believing that understanding a concept is the same as applying it. It isn't.

Knowledge without action produces little change.

But even one small action, repeated consistently over time, can completely transform the future of a family.

That is why I want to leave you with a simple challenge.

## Don't Try to Change Everything Today

You do not need to become a financial expert overnight.

You do not need to eliminate every debt this week.

You do not need to own multiple businesses by next month.

You do not need to make six figures before beginning your journey.

You simply need to take the next wise step.

Small decisions, made consistently, often produce extraordinary results.

The future you desire will not be built in one dramatic moment.

It will be built through ordinary choices repeated faithfully over many years.

## Choose Your First Step

As you close this book, ask yourself:

What is the one financial decision I need to make today?

Perhaps your first step is:

- Creating your first monthly budget.
- Opening a savings account.
- Building an emergency fund.
- Paying off your smallest debt.
- Reviewing your insurance coverage.
- Writing your will.
- Beginning your retirement savings.
- Purchasing your first investment.
- Starting a small business.
- Creating an additional stream of income.
- Teaching your child how to save.
- Scheduling a meeting with a financial professional.
- Having your first family conversation about money.

No step is too small if it moves you forward.

Progress is always more valuable than procrastination.

## Become the Turning Point

Perhaps you come from a family where money was never discussed.

Perhaps debt has been part of your family's story for generations.

Perhaps no one taught you how to invest, save, or build wealth.

Perhaps you have made financial mistakes that still weigh heavily on your heart.

If so, remember this:

Your past does not have to become your family's future.

Every family tree has someone who changes its direction.

Someone decides to think differently.

Someone decides to learn.

Someone decides to plan.

Someone decides to build.

Someone decides to break unhealthy cycles.

Why shouldn't that person be you?

You may never know how many lives will be changed because you chose to begin today.

## Think Beyond Your Lifetime

Imagine your grandchildren opening the doors to opportunities that began with one decision you made.

Imagine them graduating from university because you established an education fund.

Imagine them inheriting a thriving family business.

Imagine them managing investments with confidence because you taught them financial wisdom.

Imagine them becoming generous leaders because they watched your example.

Your decisions today may echo through generations you will never meet.

That is the extraordinary power of intentional living.

## Remember What Matters Most

As you continue your financial journey, never lose sight of what true wealth really means.

True wealth is not measured by luxury.

It is measured by freedom.

By peace.

By opportunity.

By wisdom.

By generosity.

By integrity.

By the strength of your family.

By the lives you influence.

Money is important.

But money alone has never been the greatest legacy.

The greatest legacy is a life that equips others to flourish.

## My Hope for You

It is my sincere hope that this book becomes more than something you read once and place on a shelf.

I hope it becomes a guide you return to whenever you need encouragement, direction, or a reminder of the vision you have for your family.

I hope these principles spark meaningful conversations around your dinner table.

I hope they inspire children to dream bigger, parents to plan wiser, and families to build stronger foundations together.

Most of all, I hope they remind you that no matter where you begin, your future can be different from your past.

Every wise decision you make is another investment in the legacy you are creating.

## Continue the Journey

Learning is only the beginning.

Building requires action.

That is why I created the Generational Wealth Planner as a practical companion to this book.

Inside the planner, you will find guided exercises, financial assessments, budgeting tools, savings trackers, debt reduction plans, investment worksheets, retirement planning pages, family legacy activities, and annual reviews designed to help you apply the principles you have learned.

The planner transforms ideas into habits.

Habits into progress.

Progress into wealth.

And wealth into legacy.

My encouragement is simple:

Don't close this book and say,

*"One day I'll get started."*

Close this book and say,

**"Today is the day I begin."**

Because the future of your family is not determined by chance.

It is shaped by the decisions you make today.

And perhaps, years from now, your children and your children's children will look back and recognize this moment as the day everything began.

## A Final Blessing

May you have the wisdom to manage well what has been entrusted to you.

May you have the discipline to remain faithful in both seasons of abundance and seasons of challenge.

May your home be filled with peace rather than financial anxiety.

May your work produce meaningful opportunities.

May your generosity bless others.

May your family grow in wisdom, unity, and purpose.

May your children inherit not only financial resources but also integrity, compassion, faith, and the courage to build upon the foundation you have established.

And may the legacy you leave become a blessing that reaches far beyond your own lifetime.

Your story is still being written.

Your legacy is still being built.

Your first step begins today.

Now... go build something that will outlive you.

# Generational Wealth Planner Companion

## Welcome to the Next Step

Congratulations on completing *A Beginner's Guide to Generational Wealth*. By finishing this book, you have taken an important step toward changing your financial future. But lasting transformation doesn't come from information alone—it comes from consistent action.

The **Generational Wealth Planner** was created to help you turn the principles you've learned into daily habits, measurable goals, and long-term results. Think of this book as your guide and the planner as your personal roadmap.

## How to Use the Planner

The planner includes:

✔ Financial Vision

✔ Annual Goals

✔ Monthly Budgets

✔ Cash Flow

✔ Debt Reduction

✔ Savings Goals

✔ Asset Building

✔ Retirement Planning

✔ Family Legacy

✔ Wealth Reflection

You are encouraged to complete one section at a time rather than rushing through it.

## The Seven Pillars of Generational Wealth

| Pillar | Planner Section |
|---|---|
| Vision | Family Legacy Vision |
| Mindset | Money Mindset Assessment |
| Discipline | Budget, Savings & Cash Flow |
| Ownership | Asset Tracker |
| Protection | Insurance & Estate Planning |
| Multiplication | Income Streams Planner |
| Legacy | Family Mission & Legacy Letter |

## Your 90-Day Wealth Action Plan

**First 30 Days**

- Complete your Wealth Vision.
- Create your budget.
- Track spending.
- Start an emergency fund.

**Days 31–60**

- Begin debt reduction.
- Increase savings.
- Review insurance.
- Research one investment.

**Days 61–90**

- Create another income stream.
- Build your asset plan.
- Hold your first family money meeting.

- Write your Legacy Letter.

---

**Annual Wealth Review**

You are encouraged to revisit the planner every year.

Ask questions like:

- Did I increase my net worth?
- Did I reduce debt?
- Did I increase my savings?
- Did I acquire a new asset?
- Did I create another income stream?
- Did I teach my children something new about money?
- Am I closer to the legacy I envisioned?

This reinforces that generational wealth is built over years, not weeks.

---

# A Personal Message from the Author

My hope is that this planner becomes more than a place to record numbers. I hope it becomes a record of transformation—of dreams becoming plans, plans becoming action, and action becoming legacy. Every goal you achieve, every debt you eliminate, every dollar you save, and every lesson you pass on brings you one step closer to changing your family's future.

Remember, generational wealth is not built in a single moment. It is built one faithful decision at a time.

**Sherique Simms-Dill**

Author, Educator & Generational Wealth Advocate

# ABOUT THE AUTHOR

SHERIQUE C. SIMMS-DILL is an author, educator, content creator, and Senior Executive Secretary with more than twenty years of professional experience. *Created to Stand Out Not Fit In* is her debut book—the one that launched her writing career and set her on a journey of inspiring others through words. What began as a bold message of courage and authenticity blossomed into a powerful writing path that continues to impact lives across the world.

Since its release, Sherique has gone on to publish a diverse range of books, including:

- *A Cage Called Job* – a bold reflection on breaking free from limiting systems
- *How to Become a Master of Self* – a guide to personal mastery and discipline
- *Harmony in Verses* – a heartfelt collection of poetry
- *A Throne Reclaimed: Nzingae and Zabu's Battle for the Crown* – an imaginative fiction novel weaving courage and legacy
- *Her Wealth in Coins* – a personal and financial empowerment journey (Coming soon)
- *The Sacred Female, The Divine Feminine* – an exploration of feminine

wisdom, cycles, and empowerment (Coming soon)

Her passion for teaching also led her to create international online courses in leadership, professional development, and personal empowerment. Her offerings include *Steps to Becoming an Effective Leader in Your Workplace*, *A Simple Guide to Setting Goals*, *Developing Quality Customer Service*, *Professional Secretary and Minute Taking Skills: Your Path to Office Excellence*, *Secretarial Studies and Office Administration*, *Mastering Meeting Minutes*, *Time Management for Office Professionals*, and *Mastering Your Income Effectively*.

As her journey continues, Sherique is embracing a new author identity under her pen name **Seraphine Ina Cherie**, which will carry forward her future books and creative works. Readers of her earlier works will always recognize her signature voice—bold, empowering, and transformational—now expressed through her new name.

**This revised and expanded edition reflects years of additional research, teaching, and practical experience in financial education and legacy building.**

## Don't miss out!

Visit the website below and you can sign up to receive emails whenever Sherique Dill publishes a new book. There's no charge and no obligation.

https://books2read.com/r/B-A-FJHZ-DVFLC

BOOKS 2 READ

Connecting independent readers to independent writers.

www.ingramcontent.com/pod-product-compliance
Lightning Source LLC
LaVergne TN
LVHW100322210926
848480LV00003B/1224
* 9 7 9 8 2 3 3 5 8 8 9 2 1 *